COURT JESTERS

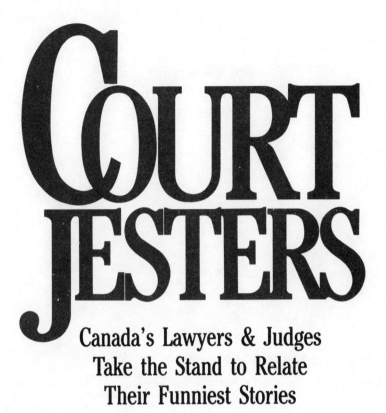

COURT JESTERS

Canada's Lawyers & Judges
Take the Stand to Relate
Their Funniest Stories

Peter V. MacDonald, Q.C.
Illustrations by David Brown

METHUEN
Toronto New York London Sydney Auckland

For Catherine,
Michael, Shaun
and Mary

Canadian Cataloguing in Publication Data

MacDonald, Peter V. (Peter Vincent), 1934–
  Court jesters

ISBN 0-458-99450-2

1. Courts — Canada — Anecdotes, facetiae,
satire, etc. 2. Law — Canada — Anecdotes,
facetiae, satire, etc. I. Title.

K184.7.C3M33 1985   347.71′01′0207   C85-099024-6

Printed and bound in the United States
5 6 7 8 9   89 88 87 86

Contents

ACKNOWLEDGEMENTS   *7*

FOREWORD   *9*

INTRODUCTION   *11*

PART ONE
Order in the Court   21

1
The Best Free Show in Town   22
2
Here Come de Judge   41
3
Twelve Good and True   54
4
Witnesses   59
5
Oh, Those Witty Lawyers!   75
6
They Should of Stood in Bed   86
7
This and That   93
8
Boys Will Be Boys   108

PART TWO
Yesteryear   117

9
Frontier Justice   118

10
The Fastest Wit in the West *128*
11
A.B. *142*
12
"Justice — With Costs" *153*

PART THREE
Hearsay *165*

13
Pardon the Pun *166*
14
Oops! *178*
15
Stupid Questions *185*
16
Words *191*

P.S. *203*
CONTRIBUTORS *204*

Acknowledgements

Thanks are certainly in order. But where does a guy start?

Well, for openers, I suppose Adam and Eve should take a bow. If they hadn't gotten together, my parents wouldn't have, either, and the world would have had to muddle along without *Court Jesters*. Perish the thought!

Much as I appreciate the aid of my antecedents, my strongest applause is reserved for my dear wife, Catherine, whose love and encouragement spurred me on. It's difficult at times to be married to a lawyer: The law is a "jealous mistress" that demands large chunks of a lawyer's time. It's equally tough to be a writer's spouse, for the same reason. Cheerfully, Catherine wore both hats. With great relish, she plunged into piles of funny mail people sent my way, helping me select the "winners" for this book. We laughed a lot together, which made us feel good all over, as laughing always does.

There were plenty of laughs for our children, too, and for my office staff – Karen Glasser, Frank and Barb Schuler, Charlotte Valles and Sheila Stephenson. My thanks to Karen and Barb for a prodigious amount of typing on a word processor I'm still trying to master, and further thanks to all five of these good folks for letting me "try out" my material on them. They shot from the hip and helped improve the product.

I greatly appreciate the encouragement I received from my mother, Hilda C. MacDonald, and from my friends Gary and Mary-Lou Dale, Bill Dawe and Stan Smith.

A special tip of the hat to Bob Holden, who had a lot to do with waking me from a long sleep.

My heartfelt thanks to Fred Wardle, Bill Hushion and Greg Cable of Methuen Publications, whose faith in this project was wondrous to behold.

Last, but by no means least, I wish to thank all the enthusiastic people who, in the short space of a year, presented me with hundreds of funny Canadian legal stories. Hard as it may be to believe, there's lots more where those yarns came from. The surface has barely been scratched.

I'll thank you to remember that.

Hanover, Ontario
May 1985

Foreword

by

John J. Robinette, Q.C.

Peter V. MacDonald, Q.C., has written an intriguing and very funny book on wit in court. Mr. MacDonald is a practising lawyer in the town of Hanover in the county of Bruce, Ontario, and he has also had extensive journalistic experience. The result is that he has been able to reproduce in a vivid and engaging style humorous incidents which have happened in courts from Newfoundland to British Columbia. He has obviously interviewed a number of people and has corresponded with many others, and in the result he has brought forth a harvest of courtroom humour which will fascinate laymen and lawyers alike.

His book is not confined to lawyers' wit which can be an effective tool of advocacy; it also includes judges, witnesses, jurymen and even the errors made by court reporters in their typewritten transcripts of evidence at a trial. The chapter headings are bright and airy and every Ontario lawyer will know who is being dealt with in the chapter entitled "Justice – With Costs," as every western lawyer will know who is covered in the chapter entitled "The Fastest Wit in the West."

Books on courtroom humour are very rare and the only book comparable in some respects to Mr. MacDonald's book is Maurice Healy's *The Old Munster Circuit*, which was written in 1914. Healy dealt only with the courts in the southwest of Ireland, whereas Peter MacDonald has achieved the onerous task of collecting stories from every province of Canada. He has produced a remarkable panorama of Canadian courtroom humour.

Peter MacDonald is a son of the late Honourable Vincent MacDonald, who was a judge of the Court of Appeal of Nova Scotia. Vincent MacDonald was a scholarly and witty man and he would be proud of his son's effort.

Introduction

When my beautiful wife awoke that morning, she stretched, yawned, rolled over in bed and bumped into a seedy-looking man. It was me, scribbling furiously in a notebook.

"What gives?" she inquired.

"I've come out of retirement."

"From what?"

"From twenty years of talking."

"Don't you mean forty-nine years? And when did you retire? I hadn't noticed – "

"Shh!" I was having a brain wave. "I'm going for the title," I announced tersely, my pen dancing across the page.

My wife eyed me curiously. "Well, *I'm* going for the doctor!" she said, reaching for the phone. "You've been working too hard and if you don't slow – "

"Hold it!" I snapped, my pen poised for the final attack. "There! I've got it!"

"Got what?"

"The title."

"But you haven't even gotten out of bed."

"No, no, my dear. The title to the book I've been talking about for twenty years. I'm going to call it *Court Jesters*."

The missus put down the phone. "Well, now you're *talking*!" she declared.

My children were also pleased to know that, at long last, the old man was going to put his typewriter where his mouth was.

"When you sell your book, will you treat me to a trip around the world?" asked sixteen-year-old Mary, who has the itchiest feet in town.

"I'll be your agent for a measly ten percent," said eighteen-year-old Shaun, an enterprising lad if ever there was one.

"Finally getting off the pot, eh, Dad?" said Michael, who was nineteen at the time.

Yes. I was finally getting off the pot.

For four interesting summers in the 1950s, I covered the courts for the Halifax *Mail-Star*. In the other seasons, I attended St. Francis Xavier University, in Antigonish, Nova Scotia, a fine institution which dealt me a Bachelor of Arts degree in 1954. A few months later, I joined the

Toronto *Globe and Mail* as a reporter, and for about half of my twenty-eight months at the paper, I covered the "legal beat," reporting the daily doings of all Toronto courts, from Magistrates' Court to the Ontario Court of Appeal.

After prolonged exposure to such forensic stars as John Robinette, Arthur Martin, Arthur Maloney, Joe Sedgwick and Charlie Dubin, to mention just a few, I decided to study law myself. I checked into the Faculty of Law at the University of Toronto, where I was fortunate to study under the illustrious Dean Cecil A. Wright and Professor Bora Laskin, later Chief Justice of Canada. I continued to do newspaper work in the summers, including two stints with the Toronto *Telegram*, and in 1962 I was called to the Bar of Ontario. After a year off for travel and magazine writing, I began practising law in Hanover, a small town in southwestern Ontario. I'm still at it.

The years zip by. It's hard for me to believe, but it's thirty-five years since I first cottoned to the fact that legal people have a lot of funny stories to tell. I don't mean "jokes," which are manufactured tales. I mean *true*, humorous stories about lawyers and judges and witnesses.

My father was Vincent C. MacDonald, who was Dean of the Faculty of Law at Dalhousie University from 1934 to 1950. In 1950 he was appointed to the Supreme Court of Nova Scotia, the first full-time law teacher in Canada to reach that position. He died in 1964 at the age of sixty-seven. Dad was a great raconteur, and so were many of his friends. When they got together at our house, explosions of laughter usually drove me from my bed to the top of the stairs, where I'd sit and listen to grown men – learned men – trying to outdo each other in the ancient and honorable art of telling stories. Sometimes I didn't understand what they were saying, but I knew it had to do with lawyers and judges and things that happened in court. What I remember most is how obviously *happy* these men were to be there, swapping stories about the law. A great joy seemed to pervade these get-togethers.

Later, I became privy to some of this stuff. The first legal story I remember was told to me by my father when I was fifteen or sixteen (the story is in this book, in the chapter on Magistrate A.B. MacGillivray), and before I left home for "Upper Canada" at the tender age of twenty, I was privileged to sit in on some story sessions with Dad and company. They were far more entertaining than anything I've ever seen and heard on TV talk shows – and there weren't any commercials, either.

As I became more involved in the law, I heard and appreciated more legal yarns, and I remember saying, on different occasions, that "someone should collect these stories in a book." I always assumed that someone would. But someone didn't, which is another way of saying no one did. It bothered me, but not greatly. There were too many other events to be concerned about: marks, graduation, "getting started," raising kids.

There was one night, though, when the seed was planted in my mind. That was the night that the great lawyer and suberb raconteur, Joseph Sedgwick, Q.C., spoke at our law school graduation dinner. He told one hilarious legal story after another, including some Paddy Nolan yarns recycled in these pages, and he made us realize that in addition to their entertainment value, stories such as these were an important form of history, history that, for the most part, had not been "captured" in print. I found myself hoping that someone *would* undertake the task, the sooner the better, before too many raconteurs died off.

The seed grew and, about 1963, I started to think that maybe, just maybe, *I* would tackle the job – some day. For years, it rattled around in a corner of my mind. From time to time, I mentioned it to lawyers and judges. They always showed immediate interest. Some said that if I did such a book, they would go so far as to read it. Some even said they'd buy it.

Canadians are reputed to be a dull and colourless lot. This is a bum rap, if ever there was one. This book should prove that beyond a reasonable doubt. This big, beautiful country teems with wonderful stories of the witticisms of lawyers, judges and witnesses. But, alas, relatively few of them have been jotted down for posterity. Until now.

In just twelve months, I uncovered hundreds of funny anecdotes pertaining to the Canadian legal scene. What I consider to be the best are presented here. There are so many others out there, just waiting to be discovered, that I could produce a book like this, or better, every year for several years. I will, too, if people keep sending me stories and my publisher keeps publishing them.

To obtain the stories in this book, I did relatively little travelling. I made one trip to Winnipeg (to the national convention of the Canadian Bar Association), one trip to Ottawa and six or seven trips to Toronto, which is only 110 miles from where I live. About seventy-five percent of the anecdotes were mailed to me by lawyers, judges and court reporters; I received many more funny yarns from people who phoned me long-distance, many of them readers of the column I write on legal humour in the Canadian Bar Association newspaper, *The National*. I have a vast army of enthusiastic contributors, from sea to shining sea.

What all this boils down to is that we have a great many lively, witty people in this country. Even in such crummy times as these, the sense of humour of the nation is in very good shape indeed.

"The most wasted day of all is that on which we have not laughed." So spake Sebastien Chamfort, an eighteenth-century writer and wit. He knew what he was talking about. Sometimes a chuckle or a guffaw is the only thing that saves us from slipping our trolleys. Blessed is he who delivers the line that restores our perspective.

"Without laughter, life on our planet would be intolerable," writes Steve Allen in the introduction to his book, *Funny People.* "So important is laughter to us that humanity highly rewards members of one of the most unusual professions on earth, those who make a living by inducing laughter in others. This is very strange if you stop to think of it: that otherwise sane and responsible citizens should devote their professional energies to causing others to make sharp, explosive barking-like exhalations."

There is overwhelming medical evidence that those exhalations are very, very good for one's health. U.S. writer and editor Norman Cousins used the power of laughter and thought to conquer a crippling illness. When doctors told him he was suffering from a progressively deforming arthritis of the spine, he simply refused to surrender to depression and despair. He tossed out his drugs, took up a good diet and gorged himself on laughter by watching old *Candid Camera* shows, Marx Brothers films and reading scores of humorous books. Cousins said he wasn't always happy *while* he was laughing, but happiness and relief from pain soon followed. He found that ten minutes of belly-laughing gave him an hour of pain-free sleep, and the more he laughed, the more his health improved. "Laughter is a bullet-proof vest!" he wrote.

Many writers besides Cousins have given laughter an A-1 rating. Here's a brief sampling:

"Nobody ever died of laughter." (Max Beerbohm)

"Laughter is a tranquilizer with no side effects." (Arnold Glasow)

"If you don't learn to laugh at trouble, you won't have anything to laugh at when you grow old." (Ed Howe)

"If you are not allowed to laugh in heaven, I don't want to go there." (Martin Luther, 1483–1546)

"God cannot be solemn, or he would not have blessed man with the incalculable gift of laughter." (Sydney Harris)

"It better befits a man to laugh at life than to lament over it." (Seneca, 4 B.C. – 65 A.D.)

That last chap, Seneca, might have been the inspiration for the lyricist who wrote: "Laugh and the world laughs with you, cry and you cry alone." Sooooo true. Mr. Justice Allan Wachowich, of the Alberta Court of Queen's Bench, put it nicely: "You've got to keep laughing," he told me. "If you don't, it's a rough highway."

Morris Shumiatcher, Q.C., of Regina, is one of Canada's foremost counsel. He's also an excellent writer and a witty raconteur. In his book, *Man of Law*, which I heartily recommend to anyone in or entering the legal world, Shumiatcher has some interesting observations on laughter and the law:

"There are some who say there is no place for laughter in the courtroom. I regard such people as disciples of melancholy who have lacked an experienced mentor to light their gloomy way. Even Schopenhauer justified laughter among mankind. Man's lot, he said, is so miserable, he is the only animal whom nature found it necessary to endow with the capacity to laugh.

"Every warrior has need for laughter to lighten his load. Whether he sits upon the bench or stands many years at the bar hoping to be offered a seat, the courtroom lawyer greets wit as a freshener that raises the spirit and eases the tensions of trial. An apt phrase in court can be more therapeutic than loosening shoe laces that have grown too tight after standing three hours before a demanding judge.

"As Reginald Hine, that 'un-common attorney,' confessed, 'Lawyers are not professional wits, but there is a good deal of wit flying about the profession.' So much solemnity hedges the lawyer's life – his gown, the trappings of the courtroom, the demeanor of the judge, the subject-matter of most trials – death, imprisonment and money – that it is natural for the man of law to unburden himself with frivolity and laughter . . .

"Because the courtroom is a place of grief, humour is a welcome visitor: has it not been said that laughter is God's hand upon a troubled world?"

My father, Vincent C. MacDonald, had the same serious message about humour. In an address entitled "Practical Hints for Young Lawyers," which was published in the Canadian Bar Review in 1928, he said:

"Cultivate your sense of humour. The lawyer's work is arduous and vexatious and the ability to see the humorous side of a situation or an adverse incident will prevent him from becoming a spiritless grind and keep his hope high and his vision clear. If he have no sense of humour and no touch of stoic philosophy about him he should abandon law forthwith, for he needs both."

By a strange and amusing coincidence, I have another example of

Morris Shumiatcher and Vincent MacDonald making the same important point, each in his own inimitable way.

First, Shumiatcher:

"What, then, does this ingredient called 'humour' mean to our model man of law? It is the pratfall that cracks the pretensions of the powerful and reminds everyone that, however high and exalted their chairs may be raised, all who are concerned with the law (and that includes judges, lawyers, clerks, reporters, litigants, witnesses, police officers and the journalists who adopt all of these as their own, yes, and those who legislate laws, and even those who bureaucratize them) all sit upon precisely the same human anatomy."

Now, MacDonald. Here's the sage advice my Dad gave me when I was leaving the nest and setting out to conquer the world:

"Son, if you ever find yourself in awe of any man – an editor, a lawyer, a judge, or anyone else – you'll keep your perspective about that person if you remind yourself that two or three times a day he goes into the bathroom, pulls down his pants and craps."

Thanks, Dad. I needed that.

Many people are surprised to learn that there's even such a thing as courtroom humour. They picture courtrooms as places of the utmost solemnity, citadels of rigid decorum where words of levity are never, ever uttered. Most courtrooms *are* very sombre places most of the time, but every now and then someone says something funny – often unintentionally – and the tension of the trial is mercifully and temporarily broken. Spontaneous moments of mirth often save a judge from sliding hopelessly into a slough of boredom. Yes, trials are often *that* dull!

One judge, in the midst of an intolerably boring case, spoke these words of deep appreciation: "The court is very much obliged to any learned gentleman who beguiles the tedium of a legal argument with a little honest hilarity."

"The element of humour that's most desired and welcomed is the element of surprise," says the Honourable Sam Freedman, former Chief Justice of Manitoba. Mr. Freedman, an extremely witty man himself, says there are fewer "characters" at the bar today than there used to be and so "things are more predictable" than in days of yore.

Judge Joseph L. Addison, who has been a magistrate and Provincial Court judge in Toronto for twenty-seven years, agrees completely.

"One thing I have noticed over the years is that humour in the courtroom has greatly diminished," he says. "When I first started, everybody in the courts drank a lot more, womanized a great deal more and were much quicker with a quip. There were a great many more characters. The magistrates were about seventy percent non-lawyers and were basically finders of fact. The Charter of Rights – if there had been such a thing – would have had no more effect on our judgements than a soft summer breeze on Gibraltar."

Does this mean conditions have deteriorated, or improved? It depends on your outlook. If you lament the decrease in spontaneous wit and "colour," you're in the same boat as Woody Allen, who noted: "Most of the time I don't have much fun. The rest of the time I don't have any fun at all."

If, on the other hand, you feel that wit and colour do not belong in court in the first place, you will herald these developments as giant steps in the right direction. I can assure you, though, from reading hundreds of letters sent to me in connection with this book, that there's still plenty of humour in our Canadian courts. Not as much as when pugnacious advocacy and ham-acting were the fashion, but more than enough to keep the nation smiling.

Lend an ear to Professor Dale Gibson of the University of Manitoba Faculty of Law:

"Whenever lawyers relax, stories are told – stories about bizarre cases, eccentric witnesses, unusual clients and remarkable colleagues; stories about tactical gaffes, brilliant ripostes and slips of the tongue; stories of wit, stories of pomposity, stories of compassion. This vast body of anecdotal lore serves many useful functions: to illustrate and perpetuate the traditions of the profession, to remind lawyers of their limitations, and to celebrate the variety and colour of the legal panoply.

"Like all mythology, this lore is for the most part transmitted verbally. But the opportunities for doing so do not arise as frequently as they did in a more leisured age. It is therefore more important now than it once was to record as much as possible in permanent form."

Right on, Professor! With raconteurs dropping off like flies, taking their tales with them, there's a pressing need to capture as many of these stories as possible for posterity. I beseech knowledgeable parties to send me their humorous Canadian legal anecdotes with "all deliberate speed" and, in the meantime, I invite them to feast on those that are presented here.

Witnesses, you will note, deliver many of the best punchlines. Usually, they don't mean to. The Honourable G.A. Gale, former Chief Justice of Ontario, throws light on the subject:

"Lawyers are involved in an adversarial system whereby they're fighting cases against other lawyers. Lay people involved in those cases are out of their element. They're not attuned to their setting, and they'll say things that are perfectly natural to them but extremely amusing to others."

Many legal anecdotes are told and retold, embellished and re-embellished. As one writer has noted, "Human memory, particularly when based on hearsay, is fallible. Some of the best legal stories have gone the long rounds and gathered dust. Frequently they are attributed to a great many different people."

The "arse pocket" story, which appears in the chapter on Magistrate A.B. MacGillivray, is a perfect case in point. It was the first anecdote contributed to this book. In Nova Scotia it's always attributed to MacGillivray, a flamboyant and humorous magistrate who presided in Glace Bay from 1894 to 1941. The story goes as follows:

Magistrate A.B. MacGillivray convicted a smart-aleck on a charge laid by the town police.

"I'm fining you twenty-five dollars . . . " A.B. said.

"No problem, Your Worship, I've got that in me arse pocket."

" . . . and sentencing you to thirty days in the County Jail. Have you got *that* in your arse pocket?"

If Magistrate MacGillivray uttered those famous words (and all indications are that he did), he must have swiped them from Sir Matthew Baillie Begbie, who made the same crack many years earlier on the other side of the country. Begbie, British Columbia's first Supreme Court judge, presided from 1857 to 1894.

In his biography of Begbie, *The Man for a New Country*, Duncan, B.C. lawyer David R. Williams, Q.C., tells of the troubles American miners brought with them when they crossed "the Line" into B.C. He relates this story:

"Begbie addresses a man convicted of assault. 'Prisoner, I am given to understand that you come from the other side of the Line. When you come to this side you must behave yourself. We will not put up with any of your bullying. I shall fine you one hundred dollars.'

" 'That's all right, Judge, I've got that in my breeches' pocket.'

" 'And six months' imprisonment with hard labour. Perhaps you have that in the other pocket!' came like a crack of a whip from the Bench."

Williams has uncovered evidence indicating that the same punchline, or one very similar to it, was delivered by judges in Missouri and California. "It may be," Williams writes, "that a California miner coming to British Columbia imported this amusing vignette, and on hearing or seeing Begbie typified him by recounting it to his friends, whereupon it passed into mythology."

That story sure gets around. In the last few months, I've received letters stating that that punchline was delivered by the local magistrate in:

- Souris, Prince Edward Island (drunk in a public place);
- Minto, New Brunswick (assault);
- Rimouski, Quebec (speeding);
- Walkerton, Ontario (drinking in public);
- Lethbridge, Alberta (possession of home brew).

In one case, it was just a "pocket," in another it was an "ass pocket," but in three cases it was an "arse pocket."

May I have the envelope? The winner is – "Arse Pocket!"

Yes, stories *do* get around. In the chapter called "Here Come De Judge!" there's an anecdote about Mr. Justice Allan Wachowich, of the Alberta Court of Queen's Bench, relating how he dealt with a man who called him a filthy name in court. Years later a member of the Supreme Court of Canada complimented him on how he handled the situation. "I asked him where he had heard the story and he said Newfoundland," His Lordship reports. "News travels a long way."

I hope news of this book travels a long way, too.

I'm honoured to be associated in this venture with the legendary John J. Robinette, Q.C. His good friend and former opponent, Mr. Justice John Arnup of the Ontario Court of Appeal, recently described Mr. Robinette as "the premier advocate" and "the giant of the Canadian bar." He truly is. And to think that he'd write the foreword for me, a boy author!

I asked my wife and kids to show proper respect for me, now that I've written a book. I suggested that when I walk into a room they should stand and shout: "Author! Author!"

Just to be contrary, they sat down and muttered: "Arthur! Arthur!"

Now I know what Sir Winston Churchill meant when he penned these words: "Writing a book is an adventure: to begin with it is a toy, then an amusement, then it becomes a mistress, and then it becomes a master, and then it becomes a tyrant, and the last phase is that just as you are about to be reconciled to your servitude you kill the monster and strew him about to the public."

That's *exactly* how I felt, and feel.

I'm killing the monster by starting to create another one – "hair of the dog" and all that – and I'm moments away from strewing this one about to the public.

Are you ready? Here it is, compliments of the Arthur!

PART ONE

Order in the Court

1

The Best Free Show in Town

Are you tired of eating the same old food all the time? Do you long for something new and different?

Why not eat your shorts?

That's what David Zurfluh did, and when word of this escaped from an Alberta courtroom, in March of 1985, it sent waves of therapeutic laughter across a nation caught in the grip of the winter blahs.

Zurfluh, an eighteen-year-old from Stettler, Alberta, was nabbed by the R.C.M.P. after he fled from his car, which had been seen weaving down a highway. The Mounties put him in a patrol car, took him to a breathalyzer machine for some breathing exercises and ended up charging him with impaired driving. He pleaded not guilty and was acquitted because the breath analysis showed his blood-alcohol level exactly at the legal limit.

Constable Bill Robinson told Judge David P. MacNaughton that he "heard some ripping and tearing" from the back of the police vehicle. "I looked in the back and he was tearing pieces of the crotch of his underwear out and stuffing them in his mouth," Robinson testified. "At one point I thought he had possibly had a small stash of drugs down the front of his pants, so at that point I thought we'd go back to the office and when we got there we'd search to see what we found.

"When we got back to the office I searched him, found the material of his shorts to be missing around the crotch area and no drugs or anything of that nature. A later search was done of the police car. There were no materials found so he must have ingested his underwear. . . . Later during a conversation it was found that he believed that the ingestion of cotton underwear would absorb the alcohol in his blood."

There followed this zippy exchange between prosecutor and policeman:

Q. And, sir, how long have you been with the Royal Canadian Mounted Police?

A. Going on seven years, sir.

Q. And, sir, have you had experience in dealing with impaired drivers on prior occasions?

A. Yes, sir, many times.

Q. And has eating one's shorts ever gone on before?

A. No, I've never had anyone eat their underwear.

Q. And did you consider that to be usual or unusual behaviour?

A. I considered that to be very unusual behaviour, sir.

Students from a local high school, in court to view the law in action, roared with laughter when they heard the evidence. When they couldn't stop laughing, they were removed by their teacher.

"People were leaving the courtroom with tears in their eyes," said a Mountie who showed the same symptoms.

Ah, court. The best free show in town! You never know what's going to be said or done. Usually no one says or does anything funny, but there's always the chance that someone – judge, lawyer, witness – will oblige. You have to expect the unexpected.

The first time I ever set foot in a courtroom, all hell broke loose. It was July of 1951, I was a seventeen-year-old cub reporter on the Halifax *Mail-Star*, and I was sitting at the press table in "Police Court" as an observer.

A few minutes after court began, a man appeared before Magistrate Jeff Flinn, charged with stealing a pair of shoes. He had tried the shoes on, walked around the store to see how they fit and had kept going. He was caught a few blocks away.

The man pleaded guilty to the charge and I recall him saying something about wanting to see his mother in Charlottetown. I remember that Magistrate Flinn, who had just taken a squint at the accused's lengthy record, said: "You'll see your mother after you've served six months!"

The man went berserk and shouted, "I want *two years*! I want *two years*!"

He upended a large desk on Police Sergeant Roy Montague, sending Roy on his keester, spilling ink all over him and scaring him half to death. He ranted and raved about wanting to go to penitentiary to learn a trade, and when a policeman grabbed him he started fighting. It took five or six officers to subdue him.

The man could have escaped by doing a swan dive over the press table and through the open window behind me, but he was too busy scrapping with police to try. I'm glad, too, because I could have been hurt. That sort of thing is against my religion. I'm a devout coward.

I was reminded of this incident recently when I saw a news story about a man who burst into an Edmonton courtroom and fired an egg at a judge. He missed. The man was tackled by three policemen, and the judge then said to the audience: "I hope that does away with all the unsatisfied customers."

There were plenty of "unsatisfied customers" in a Vancouver courtroom on February 24, 1961. That was the day that Mr. Justice A.M. Manson sang his "swan song." And what a song it was!

Mr. Justice Manson, known throughout British Columbia as "the hanging judge," was appearing in court for the last time. He'd been forced into bitter retirement by a new law which compelled federally appointed judges to retire when they reached age seventy-five. He was well past the limit.

A young man named Grant, who'd been convicted of rape, appeared before His Lordship for sentencing. He was sentenced to twenty-five years.

Next came a youth named Muggli – the last person ever to appear before the dreaded Mr. Justice Manson. Muggli, age eighteen, had been convicted of what his prosecutor later called "the very gentle rape" of a young woman. The jury's verdict was an unusual one: "Guilty with a very strong recommendation for leniency as according to the evidence there was insufficient resistance by the complainant."

Vancouver lawyer Nick Mussallem spoke eloquently on behalf of Muggli, but in his last judicial act Mr. Justice Manson ignored all pleas, including the special recommendation of the jury, and sent Muggli away for fifteen years.

As soon as sentence was passed, Muggli's mother leaped to her feet in the back of the courtroom and peppered the judge with invective. "You miserable, rotten, sadistic old bastard! You old bag of shit! You ought to be shot, you . . . "

Mr. Justice Manson listened impassively to this outburst, then directed that Mrs. Muggli be removed from the courtroom. Court orderlies hustled her offstage.

Before court, it had been agreed that Crown Counsel George Murray (now Mr. Justice Murray) should say a few words to His Lordship to mark his last day on the bench. With easy eloquence, Murray gave the valediction, paying tribute to a "fearless and forthright judge" who had "the courage of his convictions." Indeed, he said, "no one could ever deny that Your Lordship has been a very courageous judge."

"I associate myself with the remarks of my learned friend," assistant prosecutor John Davies said. Then he sat down.

"I associate myself with the remarks of both my learned friends," said Dave Sturdy, who had acted for the lad who was given twenty-five years. Then he too sat down.

"I associate myself with the remarks of all my learned friends," said Muggli's lawyer, Nick Mussallem. Then he sat down.

"And I associate myself with the remarks of Mrs. Muggli," said court reporter Don Smith as he strolled out of court.

Mr. Justice Manson bowed and left the bench forever.*

Yes, sir, you don't know what you'll see or hear in court. Take the case of Claude Hamel, which came to me via the man who prosecuted it, Rod McLeod, Q.C., who these days serves as Deputy Solicitor General of Ontario.

In the late 1960s and early 1970s, Claude Hamel, a large man who lived in a rural shack with his wife and six children, travelled all over Ontario seeking donations for a camp for under-privileged children. To facilitate matters, he appointed himself "Archbishop of the Old Roman Catholic Church" – a figment of his fertile imagination – and decked himself out in gaudy clerical robes. He purported to be associated with several other nonexistent help-the-kids organizations, too, and he actually *was* a member of "the Church of Satan" in California.

On his travels, Hamel carried a looseleaf binder containing photographs of the alleged camp. In fact, they were pictures of his own shabby home, and all the monies he collected went to support the wife and

---

* *Nick Mussallem took the Muggli case to the British Columbia Court of Appeal, winning a new trial on a number of grounds, not the least of which was that there were 800 interruptions by Mr. Justice Manson in 270 pages of transcript. The trial before Mr. Justice Manson was the second time Muggli had been tried for "the very gentle rape." An earlier trial had resulted in a hung jury. There was no third trial: the complainant had married and moved away and she had no wish to testify again.*

Grant, who'd received twenty-five years, appealed his conviction, too. The Court of Appeal quashed the conviction, stating that the evidence against him had been weak and unreliable. The Crown decided not to have a new trial and Grant, as they say, "walked."

kids and, of course, Daddy himself. He needed a fair bit to finance his trips, to nourish his six-foot, 250-pound body and to keep him in long, flowing robes, bright sashes and such accoutrements as gold chains and crosses to wear under his long, flowing beard.

He had a long, flowing time of it, bilking businessmen hither and yon, but one day the coppers nailed him and in due course he was obliged to travel to Toronto to face judge and jury.

Rod McLeod was ready for him. He had forty businessmen, from all over the province, waiting to testify as to how the "Archbishop" had swindled them.

But while he awaited trial, Hamel had shed fifty or sixty pounds, and he showed up in court looking trim and fit and minus his beard, robes, chains and sashes.

McLeod made his opening speech to the jury, then called his first witness, the proprietor of a small variety store in Oshawa.

"Please look around the courtroom and tell the Court whether you see the person who solicited funds from you," the prosecutor instructed the witness.

The witness started on his left, gazing intently at each member of the jury. Next, his eyes travelled to the counsel table and rested briefly on each lawyer and assistant sitting there. He scrutinized the investigating policeman, who was sitting beside McLeod, took a good look at the accused sitting calmly in the dock, then moved on to the press table and peered at the reporters.

Finally, the witness swung his eyes around to the bench, where he beheld a bulky man with a goatee, attired in a black gown with a purple sash. He looked into the eyes of His Honour Judge William Rogers, jabbed a finger at him and declared, "That's him!"

It was "judgement summons" day in County Court in Winnipeg. A man had been ordered to appear and explain why he'd failed to pay a judgement awarded by the court. A court official opened the door to the hallway and called his name:

"Mr. – !"

"Yes, sir?"

"Come in and take the stand."

The witness was sworn in and Judge "Bo" Macdonell started asking him questions.

"How much do you earn, Mr. – ?"

The witness mentioned a small amount.

"Well, that's not very much, but don't you think you could manage to pay Mr. Jones a few dollars every month?"

"Why should I do that?"

"Because you owe him a lot of money!"

"Oh, no, Your Honour, I don't even know a Mr. Jones."

"Well, this court has found that you both know him and owe him."

"Your Honour, there must be some mistake."

"No mistake. This order I have in front of me clearly states that you, Lawrence P. – , owe the sum of $1,240.75 to Samuel S. Jones."

"But, Your Honour, I'm not Lawrence P. – . I'm Lawrence R. – ."

"Well, what on earth are you doing here?"

"I don't really know, Your Honour. I'm a law student and I was just going out for coffee when someone called my name."

An isolated sort of occurrence, that foul-up? No. To keep things interesting, there's a comedy of errors every now and then. For example, take what happened in Cranbrook, British Columbia. On November 16, 1966, the undefended divorce case of Erik Forsberg versus Esmerelda Forsberg and Duncan O'Hoolihan was supposed to take place in Cranbrook. It didn't.

Presiding was His Honour, Judge Michelangelo Provenzano. Appearing for the plaintiff was Fred W. Barry.

All right, grab your popcorn and let's have a look at the videotape:

THE CLERK: I call the case of Forsberg and Forsberg.

MR. BARRY: I call Mr. Forsberg.

THE COURT: Please don't whisper to a witness when he has been sworn in, Mr. Barry.

MR. BARRY: Well, Your Honour, I think that . . .

THE COURT: If you have anything to say to him say it so that we can all hear it.

MR. BARRY: Witness, you have told me this morning that a witness you hoped to bring here to corroborate is some twenty-five miles north of Revelstoke and he isn't here.

THE WITNESS: No, I think there is a little bit of confusion here, Your Honour. I am sorry but . . .

THE COURT: Sit down, sit down.

THE WITNESS: . . . I don't understand what is going on myself.

THE COURT: I beg your pardon?

THE WITNESS: I don't understand what is going on myself.

THE COURT: You don't understand what is going on? You initiated these proceedings, you instituted these proceedings. Surely you should know what is going on. You instructed your solicitor to start a divorce action against your wife.

THE WITNESS: I am afraid not. I am separated from my wife but I mean this . . . this has no bearing on this court action whatever. I am not here for that. I am here on a muffler charge.

THE COURT: Are you Erik Forsberg?

THE WITNESS: I am George Forsberg.

THE COURT: Have I got things wrong, Mr. Barry? Mr. Booth? You have called the case of Erik Forsberg versus Esmerelda Forsberg and Duncan O'Hoolihan. Is that right?

MR. BOOTH: Yes.

THE COURT: And your name is what?

THE WITNESS: George Forsberg.

THE COURT: George?

THE WITNESS: Forsberg.

THE COURT: Forsberg?

THE WITNESS: Yes.

THE COURT: F-O-R-

THE WITNESS: S-B-E-R-G.

THE COURT: Is he a witness in the Forsberg case, Mr. Barry?

MR. BARRY: No.

THE WITNESS: I misunderstood the name. I thought they called George Forsberg out, instead of this.

THE COURT: You should breathe a little easier . . . (interrupted by laughter)

THE COURT: Mr. Barry, are you ready to go on with Forsberg versus Forsberg?

MR. BARRY: It doesn't sound like it, Your Honour. Is Mr. Forsberg in the court right now? May I look out the door to see if he is outside? I would ask for an adjournment if you don't mind, My Lord.

THE COURT: Just off the record, I think we should tell Mr. Forsberg if he is up on a muffler charge he isn't in the right courtroom. Mr. Forsberg, are you supposed to be in Police Court? Where are you supposed to be?

MR. FORSBERG: Well, I don't know. I went to Court yesterday on the charge here which was supposed to be over in that court and I phoned down to the R.C.M.P. and they said they knew nothing about it and told me to come down here today. This is where they told me to come so I don't know exactly myself what is going on.

THE COURT: Maybe Mr. Worley. . . .

MR. WORLEY: I will assist him in where he has to go.

THE COURT: If you could assist this man before he is arrested.
(Forsberg v. Forsberg adjourned until 7th December.)

On another occasion, the aforementioned lawyer, Fred Barry, defended a man charged with murder. The judge summed up the evidence for the jury. When he reached the part that hurt the accused the most, Barry, anxious to distract the jurors from hearing what he preferred them not to hear, started to brush his teeth at the counsel table. A "judicial explosion" ensued.

We travel now to the Northwest Territories for another story of a man who was paged to come into court.

The late, legendary Mr. Justice William Morrow was presiding at a criminal trial in a community hall in the far, far north. The accused, an Inuit man, had, as they say, "gone missing."

His Lordship asked the court clerk to go to the door and call the accused in the usual way.

The clerk opened the door and cried out: "Wandering Spirit! . . . Wandering Spirit! . . . Wandering Spirit!"

Attention, *Star Trek* fans! Regina lawyer John Epp has a gripping tale for you.

Three or four years ago, a young man pleaded guilty in a Regina courtroom to a charge of possession of marijuana. Before passing sentence, the judge delivered a lengthy sermon on the dangers of drugs, then asked the accused if he had anything to say.

The accused pulled his wallet from his back pocket, flipped it open, held it in front of his mouth and said in a loud voice:

"Scotty, beam me up!"

Around the same time, 3,000 miles away in Newfoundland, a similar drama unfolded. It was witnessed by Judge Seamus B. O'Regan, of the District Court of Newfoundland, before he went on the Bench. He sends this report:

"A young, long-haired university student had been convicted for having 'in his possession' a rather substantial amount of grass. It was obvious that the trial judge would have preferred to have convicted him of trafficking had the Crown been able to prove the offence. From the demeanor of the accused, it was obvious that he was treating the matter rather lightly.

"Having entered conviction, but before passing sentence, the judge hinted at the fact that he was considering a custodial term. He asked the accused if he had anything to say before the passing of what appeared to be a rather harsh sentence.

"Realizing his predicament, the accused looked down, unzipped his jacket, poked his head inside, and in a voice loud enough for the whole courtroom to hear, said:

" 'Hurry up, Scottie! Beam me up!' "

There must be more space cadets out there than I thought. Gail McGilvray, a London, Ontario, court reporter, sends the following down-to-earth communiqué from her home town:

"CROWN COUNSEL (ON A SHOW-CAUSE APPLICATION): The information we have from the accused is that he arrived here three months ago, on a lunar module, and he was working undercover as a secret agent. His family apparently lives in London and he is allowed access to their home to eat but he is required to sleep in a chair in an aunt's backyard. There are a number of circumstances which require further investigation. I would ask for a three-day remand to show cause.

"DUTY COUNSEL (AFTER CONFERRING WITH ACCUSED): Your Honour, I appear on behalf of the accused as (legal aid) duty counsel. He tells me that that statement by the Crown is accurate, except it was five months ago he arrived, not three."

For another story of a missile hurtling through space, we go to Halifax, Nova Scotia, where an old friend of mine, Charles W. MacIntosh, Q.C., was performing in court. We get this report from correspondent Donald A. Kerr, Q.C., who was right in the thick of things:

"One beautiful summer's day, many years ago, Charlie was addressing a Supreme Court judge, in one of the cavernous courtrooms in the old Spring Garden Road Courthouse, on some point of law. In the course of his argument, he read a passage from a rather obscure Canadian legal textbook.

" 'You know, Mr. MacIntosh,' said His Lordship, 'I never thought much of that book.'

" 'My Lord, I entirely agree,' said Charlie, upon which he wheeled around and, with the unerring aim of a Sandy Koufax, threw the offending text right out the open window."

Lawyer Charles A. Manning performed the same feat, one balmy spring day about twenty years ago, at the Court House in Pictou, Nova Scotia. While arguing a negligence case, Manning glanced over at the arsenal of books in front of his opponent, Ken Matthews, Q.C. Without so much as a "by your leave," he extracted one of Ken's books, the English text, *Kemp & Kemp on Damages*, and started quoting from it.

Judge Welsford MacDonald interrupted. "Mr. Manning, I have a great respect for English jurisprudence. However, I don't believe that English authority should be followed as to quantum of damages."

Manning paused, looked at the judge and said, "I agree." Then he pitched the borrowed tome through the open window, just as cleanly as if it had been ace hurler Charlie MacIntosh on the mound. For a while there, at least in Nova Scotia, lawbook-throwing showed signs of becoming a new athletic event.

Client-bashing gained some local fame for Rudy Kominek, a lawyer in Waterloo, Ontario. One day, back in the late 1960s, Rudy had a case before his good friend Ross Fair, who had just been appointed to the Ontario Provincial Court (Family Division). It was Judge Fair's first case.

As the curtain rose, Kominek's client, an extremely irate husband, was threatening to bop his wife in open court. He made a lunge for her and the brand-new judge spoke his first words from the bench:

"Mr. Kominek, control your client!"

Rudy clamped an arm around the husband and said: "For God's sake, shut up!"

The client started ranting and raving.

"Try to control your client, Mr. Kominek!" the judge repeated.

The lawyer forgot himself for a moment and exclaimed:

"God damn it, Ross, what do you *think* I'm doing?"

The man continued to shout and jump around. His counsel reared back and slugged him.

"I gave him a quick right to the chops," Rudy reminisced recently.

The client slumped over his chair, stopped cold by a technical knockout in the third round. He was taken off to see a shrink.

A man appearing before Judge A.P. Catonio, of the Alberta Provincial Court (Family Division), had to justify his failure to make payments to his wife.

The man rattled off his debts and said smugly that he was quite broke, adding with a smile, "You can't get blood out of a stone, Sir."

Judge Catonio asked a few more questions and then the man's nose started to bleed.

"I see that some stones *do* bleed," His Honour said as he ordered a stiff payment.

Another Alberta man, a speeder, also had a lot of explaining to do. Police radar had clocked him going ninety miles an hour through a small town near Edmonton. The judge asked him if he had an explanation. He sure did.

"I was out at Lake Wabamun," he said. "The local police pulled a dead man out of the lake who, obviously, had been floating for a long time. The police didn't have an ambulance. They put the decomposed body in the back of my station wagon and told me to get it to the City Hospital as quickly as I could. I rolled down my windows and drove as fast as the car would go."

The story checked out and the man was acquitted.

Back in the days when breathalyzer readings were not part and parcel of every impaired driving prosecution, an interesting drama was enacted in a Newfoundland courtroom.

A police witness rhymed off the usual list of complaints: "The accused's breath smelled of alcohol, his speech was thick, his eyes appeared glassy."

Defence counsel pointed out that there was no evidence as to how much his client had had to drink. He also demonstrated that the accused man's normal speech was rather thick. Then he turned to his client and said, "I believe you have something you'd like to show the court."

The man took out his glass eye and made a big production out of polishing it.

Game over for the Crown; a big victory for the defence.

County Court Judge Peter Nicholson, of Annapolis Royal, Nova Scotia, tells a heartwarming story about a lawyer, a judge and a bottle of wine. Judge Nicholson's former law partner, the late Roy Laurence, Q.C., once prosecuted a man for illegal possession of liquor – to wit, one-third of a bottle of cheap wine. The man was down on his luck and Laurence and the trial judge, Hanson T. Dowell, both felt sorry for him.

After hearing the evidence of the policeman who seized the part bottle, Judge Dowell said that, notwithstanding any presumptions raised by the Liquor Control Act, there ought to be some evidence that the fluid in the bottle was, in fact, intoxicating liquor.

Laurence agreed.

"I have some knowledge of the characteristics of intoxicating liquor," he told the judge, "and I would be glad to sample the exhibit."

Judge Dowell agreed.

Laurence drank half the contents of the bottle and announced that he had grave doubts about the matter.

"Let me have that," Judge Dowell said. "I'll settle this issue."

Laurence passed the bottle up to the judge. His Honour consumed the rest of the fluid and stated that in his opinion it had none of the characteristics of intoxicating liquor. He dismissed the charge.

Some of the situations that arise in court are so ludicrous that it's hard not to give in to the giggles. A St. Catharines, Ontario, lawyer, Ronald H. Brooks, provides an example:

A man was charged with the armed robbery of a St. Catharines convenience store. The Crown Attorney and the defence lawyer got together to review the facts. A key fact was that the bandit wore a mask – an old, soiled pair of men's underwear. The image of an armed robber peering out from the opening in a pair of putrid jockey shorts convulsed the lawyers with laughter.

The accused pleaded guilty and it was the Crown Attorney's job to read the facts aloud for the judge. He was all right until he got to the part about the underwear. Three times he tried to read out the description of the disguise, but couldn't. He broke up each time he took a stab at it. Laughter being contagious, it wasn't long before nearly everyone in court, including the judge, was laughing at the prosecutor's predicament.

Defence counsel came to the rescue. He asked for a recess so that he could discuss "an important matter" with the Crown Attorney. The prosecutor took the easy way out. When court resumed, he told the judge simply that the accused had worn a mask.

Chicken!

Ottawa lawyer Lawrence Greenspon provoked gales of laughter with an extremely short cross-examination. In a 1982 case a policeman testified that he had fingerprinted and photographed Greenspon's client. Since he admitted the man's qualifications as an identification officer, Greenspon didn't really have any questions to ask him, but he decided to have some fun.

A few weeks earlier, the lawyer had attended an evening of entertainment presented by the Ottawa Police Male Choir. The identification officer had worn a wedding dress in one of the skits.

"Officer, I understand you're a member of the Ottawa Police Force," Greenspon began.

"Yes, sir, I am."

"And either in that capacity, or any other capacity, have you ever had occasion to wear a dress?"

"Pardon?"

"Have you ever had occasion to wear a dress?"

"Yes, sir, I have."

"Okay. I have no other questions."

The courtroom rocked with laughter and it was several minutes before the witness had a chance to explain.

Some people have more nerve than Dick Tracy. Arnold Fradkin, a lawyer with the Department of Justice in Ottawa, helped prosecute a big combines case in Montreal a few years ago. He sends this report:

"A very important Crown witness was being cross-examined at great length by one of the defence counsel. There were a great many people outside the courtroom who were making a lot of noise and who could be heard by all of us inside the courtroom.

"Eventually, Mr. Justice Mackay could not tolerate it any longer and asked his attendant to ask one of the court house guards to quiet the people in the corridor because they were interfering with the testimony. The attendant left the courtroom and returned shortly thereafter.

"Nothing happened. About five minutes later, one of the guards entered the courtroom, approached the defendant's counsel who was still cross-examining the witness, and interrupted his cross-examination by tapping him on the shoulder and telling him in loud, booming tones to lower his voice because he was disturbing the conversations that were taking place outside in the corridor!"

People who have "pigged out" on Perry Mason and the like have a deep-seated belief that trials – *all* trials – sizzle with excitement from start to finish. Wrong, wrong, wrong. Most trials are dull and boring, though some do sizzle, now and then. It's *because* of the boredom that humour is such a welcome intruder.

But sometimes the only intruder – an unwelcome one, at that – is sleep. Yes, the truth of the matter is that many cases are so dull that judges have to fight like hell to keep from drifting away. Sometimes it's a losing battle. This is not too good for the administration of justice, as anyone who's not asleep can tell.

Montreal lawyer Pierre Fournier tells about a case that provided days of boredom and "a moment of irreplaceable laughter." Fournier and a colleague, Jack Miller of Montreal, "clashed" in a two-week product-liability case that was full of technical evidence and stifled yawns. Fournier's client was from New York.

Here's Fournier to tell us about the trial:

"During the first week, to our bewilderment, the learned judge started falling asleep earlier on in the day each day, so that by the end of the first week he would fall asleep almost immediately as the court was called to order.

"When Jack or I would object to the other's question, we would yell very loudly: 'I object!' – thereby waking up the judge. He would then invariably ask the reporter to repeat the question and would render his decision after hearing the question and the argument, thereupon going back to sleep.

"During the second week, we found that unfortunately the learned judge was falling asleep while the reporter was reading the question to him. Without coming to a formal agreement, Miller and I started the practice of saying, when the other was objecting, 'under reserve,' which, in the reporter's notes, eventually was translated as: '*The court*: 'Under reserve.' "

Now we come to the exciting climax. Pierre is doing so well, I'll let him finish up.

"On the final day of the hearing, Friday afternoon, about three o'clock, from a corner of the courtroom came the very loud snore of the Court Crier, who, for the first time in two weeks, not only fell asleep but fell off his chair, thereby waking up the judge.

"We were all (including the judge, who had a sense of humour) unable to continue with the trial for a good fifteen minutes as laughter grabbed us all.

"Walking out of the courtroom, my client turned to me and said: 'In our country, we picture Justice as blind. In yours, you should picture it as asleep!' "

County Court Judge Douglas MacKinnon, of Vancouver, files the following dispatch:

"Lou Mazur is a clerk-registrar in Vancouver. He is quick-witted and seldom afraid to speak his mind to anyone. Charity, not the fear of a libel suit, dictates that the judge will remain nameless.

"The trial had been lengthy. Counsel were completing lengthy submissions. It was late afternoon in a hot, stuffy courtroom. And the judge fell sound asleep!

"The lawyer addressing the court reasoned that his pearls, acquired from hours of research, were not receiving sufficient attention. He said to Mazur: 'Lou, wake up the judge!' and Lou replied, '*You* wake him up! You put the bastard to sleep!' "

Judge Walder White, Assistant Chief Judge of the Alberta Provincial Court, Family and Juvenile Divisions, tells a delightful story about a court attendant named Charlie Caldwell. Judge White, then still at the bar, was sitting in the Alberta Court of Appeal one day about 1960 while Charlie Caldwell, a big man around sixty-five years of age, sat nodding in the corner. Before long, Charlie was in the arms of Morpheus.

Charlie slumbered through a long civil appeal and when court was over his siesta wasn't.

The presiding judge, Mr. Justice Marsh Porter, thought it would be a shame to waken the attendant. He held a finger to his lips and everyone took the cue. Judges, lawyers and spectators tiptoed out of court and left Charlie snoring in the corner. By the time he awoke, everyone had gone home.

Judge White kindly lets us in on the sequel:

"Through the years in Edmonton there were many arguments between Bill Shortreed, the prosecutor, and Neil D. MacLean, a rather famous Edmonton trial lawyer. On one occasion they were arguing vociferously after leaving the courtroom. They moved into one of the side rooms and started to drink and were continuing to argue.

"Mr. Justice Neil Primrose asked Charlie Caldwell to go out and destroy the bottle, to cut down the noise. Charlie did so by drinking it. He fell asleep again."

Another sleeping-in-court story also comes to us courtesy of Judge Walder White, who sent me *fifty* funny Canadian legal anecdotes!

"In 1978, Judge Peter Levesque of the Provincial Court (Family Division) went to Gleichen, Alberta, to try cases. He was gowned, waiting to go into court, when his clerk knocked and quickly opened his courtroom door. She was white-faced and simply pointed to his Bench. Under the Bench were two feet sticking out.

"Because of a rash of murders which had already taken place in Gleichen, Judge Levesque was very concerned and immediately got the R.C.M.P. to go in and look at the situation.

"A constable went over, looked under the Bench and there was this woman, passed out completely, with her head stuck in the waste-paper basket. The constable roused her and told the Court that she was the cleaning woman.

"She staggered to her feet, started out of court and then, in the middle of the courtroom, as she was walking out, she was heard to say: 'I'm gonna quit this fucking job!' "

Hollywood scriptwriters couldn't dream up some of the true-life "sitcom" scenarios that are presented in our courts. David C. Day, Q.C., of St. John's, Newfoundland, provides a splendid example of what I mean.

Day acted for a man who suspected that his wife, a night-shift telephone operator, was cheating on him. Night after night, she returned home from work much later than usual, her clothes in disarray. Her husband hired three private detectives to follow her and, against his lawyer's advice, he tagged along.

Their sleuthing led them to a barn. While the detectives prepared to deploy an infra-red film device, the husband stole into the barn, alone. He climbed into a hayloft and peered down into a car where his wife and a man, to swipe Day's felicitous phrase, "were submitting to the urge to merge."

Attempting to get as close as he could to the action, the husband tumbled from the loft onto the hood of the car. (Talk about "coitus interruptus!") Then he fled, along with the gumshoes.

When the wife returned home that night, she made a beeline for her husband and wrestled him to the floor. She sunk her teeth through his flannel pantleg, and into his thigh, breaking off one of her front teeth.

In court a few days later, the husband, fearing that the judge didn't believe his rendition of the facts, mounted the Bench, dropped his pants and showed the three scars left by his wife's incisors.

Judge Charles Roberts imposed a "peace bond" on both warring parties and before taking leave of the case noted tersely for the record:

"This is the greatest matrimonial donneybrook I have ever witnessed."

Stuart Morrison can top that one. Morrison, an executive with Canada Law Book Company, is a former Vancouver court reporter and justice of the peace. He recalls a divorce case in which a Vancouver man came home drunk, kicked open the front door, stomped up the stairs, dragged his wife out of bed, bound her arms and legs with tape, taped her mouth shut, stuffed her into a garbage sack, carried her downstairs, put her into the trunk of his car and drove her into the country, where he freed her and had his way with her.

The courtroom was hushed while the wife reeled off these facts, which, of course, are far from funny.

The judge asked the husband, who was unrepresented, if he wished to ask his wife any questions.

"Just one," he replied.

The man looked his wife straight in the eye and asked, "But do you *love* me?"

"Oh, *yes!*" she sobbed uncontrollably, and that was the end of the trial.

And, speaking of divorce, it's time for me to blab the hitherto-unpublished story of "The Race for the New Divorce Speed Record." It's a story that's high in drama and suspense, a caper that will amuse many and, no doubt, distress others.

My source is, as journalists say, unimpeachable. He's Gordon A. Douglas, a sterling chap who runs the Vancouver office of Carswell Legal Publications, a fellow who never fibs or even gilds the lily.

The scene is Calgary, circa 1960. Young Gord Douglas is a court clerk in the Calgary Court House. Every Monday afternoon when the undefended divorce cases are presented for adjudication, Gord sits, resplendent in gown and tabs, at a desk in front of the presiding judge.

It's Monday afternoon and Gord is at his battle station. The courtroom is packed, mostly with lawyers. Many of them have no cases to present to the court. They've come for another reason. They hope to see history made. Each wants to be able to say, "I was there when it happened."

For weeks, word has been out that a certain lawyer is "going for a new record." This lawyer says he'll successfully zip an uncontested divorce case through the court faster than it's ever been done in Calgary. He's been warming up with other cases. He's become awfully fast. Two minutes faster than a year ago, some reports have it.

Uncontested divorces are pretty routine, but the lawyer has to touch all the bases. There's the testimony of two witnesses and the proper introduction and recording of three or four documents. Sure, the questions asked of the witnesses follow a set pattern, but they all must be asked. Five or six minutes usually does it. The record is two minutes and fifty-four seconds!

Mr. Justice Harold Riley is presiding today. He's a distinguished-looking man, a popular judge and a vivid "character." His Lordship knows about the record attempt. So does Gord Douglas. Indeed, he's been provided with a stop watch and dubbed "Official Time Keeper."

There are rules for this contest – "strict Olympic rules," as someone put it – and one of them is that no one, judge and clerk included, may prompt the witnesses in any way whatsoever. Like actors on the stage, the participants have cues. "You may proceed" is the signal from the judge for the clerk to start the stop watch. The rap of the gavel is the one to click it off.

"Are you ready to proceed?" Mr. Justice Riley asks the plaintiff's lawyer.

The lawyer looks to one side, sees that the plaintiff is standing at the gate and his corroborating witness is seated three feet from him.

"Yes, My Lord."

"All right. *You may proceed.*"

"Click" goes the stop watch, cupped in the clerk's right hand.

The plaintiff practically sprints to the witness box. Gord Douglas immediately swears him in. One by one, but very swiftly, the documents are presented to the plaintiff, properly identified and filed with the clerk. Rapidly, he writes the necessary words and figures on them.

Faster than a speeding bullet, the lawyer takes his client through his testimony, then dismisses him. The client strides quickly to his seat, passing the other witness on his way to the box.

Gord Douglas looks at the judge. He's the picture of dignity and serenity, but Douglas hears the judge's feet beating a fast tattoo, urging the witness on to greater speed.

The second witness is polished off so quickly he's almost a blur.

"Decree nisi," says His Lordship, rapping his gavel on the Bench.

"Click" goes the watch.

"Court is adjourned for ten minutes," the judge announces. "I'll see counsel in my chambers. You, too, Mr. Douglas."

"What was the time?" Douglas is asked as soon as he arrives backstage.

"Two minutes and thirty-nine seconds flat!"

"I *did* it! A new record!" the lawyer fairly shouts.

Gord Douglas beams. His Lordship beams, too.

But if you think that was fast work – and it certainly was – consider the performance of Ken Houston, who makes the other fellow look like a loiterer.

Kenneth G. Houston, Q.C., of Winnipeg, has what must be the all-time world speed record for proving a divorce case – a record that it's hard to imagine anyone could ever beat. For the first time in print, here's the story.

About twenty years ago, Houston wagered that he could obtain a divorce decree faster than a Winnipeg colleague, Saul Froomkin. He didn't tell Froomkin that he had already secured the evidence of a corroborating witness "on commission," that is, by having him examined beforehand and the questions and answers transcribed for the court.

Froomkin went first.

"He was so fast off the mark," Ken told me, "that he started examining the plaintiff before she'd been sworn in. This was brought to his attention and he had to start again. Poor Saul, he lost about twenty seconds right off the bat."

Froomkin whizzed around the bases, carefully touching them all, in about three and a half minutes. His client was granted a decree.

Now it was Ken's turn. The judge was "brand new" and apparently unsure of himself. It was his first day on the job, and Ken hoped he wouldn't be much of a stickler. He wasn't.

As soon as his client had been sworn in, Houston handed him the divorce petition.

"Have you read this document?" he asked.

"Yes."

"Is it correct?"

"Yes."

"I have no further questions."

Ever so quickly, the lawyer filed the commission evidence and sat down.

"Decree granted," the judge said, without further ado.

I asked Ken how long this "ordeal" had taken.

"About eleven seconds," he replied.

2

Here Come de Judge

Order in the court!

You are hereby notified that this chapter is reserved exclusively for judges. They get all the punchlines, all the laughs. Under pain of contempt of court, lawyers and witnesses may not horn in.

Judges, it should be noted, have a terribly serious job to perform. This is why many of them look terribly serious. But, believe it or not, they're all human and on occasion funny comments fall from their lips.

Yes, beneath a judge's stern exterior there often beats the heart of a comedian. Some don't show it; they fight back the temptation. A rare few aren't even tempted; they are outside the purview of this book (they probably won't even read it).

Let's drop in on some Canadian judges who, mercifully, livened the proceedings by yielding to the urge to quip. As Flip Wilson would say, "here come de judge!"

A few years ago, Vancouver lawyer J. Keith Lowes had a trial before the late Mr. Justice Victor Dryer of the British Columbia Supreme Court. A "common law" husband sued his "common law" wife for a declaration that he had a half interest in the apartment building owned by her. Both parties were "well into their seventies," Keith says, and the judge wasn't far behind them.

The man testified that he and the woman had begun to live together in their twilight years and that everything had been fine until the previous summer, when they vacationed at a local resort called Radium Hot Springs. He said he returned from a walk one day and discovered the woman in bed with an elderly man. That ended the relationship.

The woman's evidence was the same as his, in reverse. She said everything was hunky-dory until one day the previous summer, at Radium Hot Springs, when she came back from a walk and found him in the sack with an elderly woman.

Mr. Justice Dryer reserved his decision and asked to see both counsel in his chambers. As soon as they walked in he told them, "I've decided one thing already. From now on I'm going to take all my holidays at Radium Hot Springs."

In Brampton, Ontario, a few years back, Mr. Justice Sam Hughes heard the uncontested divorce case of a couple who had wed in their eighties. The husband sued for dissolution of his marriage on the ground of his wife's "mental cruelty." He said she followed the ponies and cluttered up the house with disreputable newspapers that contained the daily racing form. "This embarrassed me no end," he declared.

The last straw was drawn one evening when the man and his wife played bridge with another couple. The husband said he bid and made "three no trump" and claimed the game. His wife called him a fool and said "anyone knows it takes four no trump to make a game." The husband said he was so embarrassed that he submitted to his wife. Mr. Justice Hughes granted the divorce.

David G. Friend, Q.C., of Toronto, was in court that day and says that the very next case was a petition for divorce brought by a woman on the grounds of her husband's physical cruelty. At the start of the case, her lawyer filed documents which certified that her husband had been convicted twice of assaulting her.

Mr. Justice Hughes asked to see the certificates. He read them, looked up, smiled and said, "This sure beats three no trump."

Magistrate Martin Haley, sitting in Dartmouth, Nova Scotia, listened skeptically to the story of a witness who declared, "If I'm telling a lie, may God strike me with lightning!"

"Hit the deck!" shouted Haley, as he ducked under his desk.

Mr. Justice Allan Wachowich, of the Alberta Court of Queen's Bench, is known for his sound judgement and keen wit. Western lawyers and judges love to tell the story of the first criminal case he heard after his appointment to the Bench.

A man pleaded guilty to a charge of armed robbery and, after representations by Crown and defence counsel, the new judge announced his verdict – four years in the penitentiary. He was new at this sort of thing and, realizing that he hadn't asked the prisoner, before sentencing, if there was anything he wished to say, he asked him now.

"Yeah," the man yelled, "you're a fuckin' asshole!"

The judge could have greatly increased the sentence because of the contempt of court, but he figured this was no way to start his judicial career, so he let it ride. Still, he was reluctant to allow this foul-mouthed fellow to have the last word and as he got up to leave, the thought persisted that he should say something.

The rookie jurist paused at the door, then turned and said to the prisoner: "That, sir, was just a lucky guess!"

In another case, Mr. Justice Wachowich heard the petition of a woman who said she should be granted a divorce decree because her husband was a transvestite. A matrimonial property agreement, signed by the spouses, was filed for the approval of the court. When the evidence had been presented, His Lordship, bursting with curiosity, picked up the document and said to counsel, "I can't wait. Who gets the dresses?"

Mr. Justice Wachowich made these cryptic notes pertaining to a case he tried:

"Accused was charged with robbery with violence and the victim was William Zukowich. I gave him sixteen months and the Crown asked why such an unusual time for sentence. I said it was twelve months for the assault with violence and four months because the victim was a Polack. He said the reasoning should be the other way around."

Magistrate O.M. Martin, of Toronto, a high-school teacher before his appointment to the Bench in the 1950s, was a full-blooded Cree Indian. One day Martin sentenced a man to thirty days in prison. As he was being led off to the cells, the man said to a policeman, "Imagine, getting sent to the jug by a bloody Indian!"

The magistrate heard this crack and told the officer to bring the man back before the Bench.

"Listen here, Paleface," he told the offender. "Me Big Chief here. You go pokey thirty more days for badmouthing Big Chief!"

Les Bewley was an outspoken, controversial Provincial Court judge for years in Vancouver. Once, about to sentence a prostitute, he said to the accused, "Strange as this may sound, coming from a man, will you please stand up?"

Another Vancouver judge, about to impose sentence, said to the man in the dock, "Perhaps you'd like to say something before I sentence you. What do you want to say?"

"Fuck all!" was the angry reply.

"What did he say?" asked the judge, who was hard of hearing.

"He said 'fuck all,' " answered the court clerk.

"That's strange," the judge replied. "I was sure he said something."

Douglas S. Schofield, a Crown Attorney in Kamloops, British Columbia, prosecuted a case in 1977 in which the accused, convinced that his lack of sobriety on the day in question would assist him in his defence, repeatedly referred to himself as "pissed."

Provincial Court Judge D.R. Simpson did a slow burn, then interjected, "You have been saying 'pissed' for the last two hours now. I'm getting sick and tired of it. Is there any difference between being 'drunk' and 'pissed'? If there isn't, just use the English language, will you? I'm getting tired of that crap!"

Edmonton lawyer J.A. Matheson appeared in a divorce case in Red Deer, Alberta, in which adultery was alleged against the respondent husband. The man willingly spilled the beans. He knew the date on which he'd committed adultery, as well as the city and the area of the city where he'd sinned. But darned if he could remember the street address.

"You should remember that sort of thing," Mr. Justice Neil Primrose admonished him. "You might want to go back some day."

The late Mr. Justice Harold Riley, of the Alberta Court of Queen's Bench, was an inveterate quipster. A West Vancouver lawyer, Ronald J. Schmidt, recalls a case in which a husband sued for divorce, alleging that his wife had been mentally cruel to him. The man's lawyer struggled on for some time, trying to extract some solid evidence of mental cruelty from the petitioner, but no matter how the lawyer phrased his questions, the best he could get from his client was, "She used to . . . you know . . . bug me."

Finally, Mr. Justice Riley rode to the rescue, saying to the petitioner, "She was a nagger, wasn't she?"

"Oh, yes, My Lord!"

"Decree granted. I had one of those once."

In an Alberta paternity case, the judge, after hearing all the evidence, looked at the suspect and said: "Young man, if I were you I'd go out and buy some cigars because you're about to become a father."

A Newfoundland magistrate ruled that a certain young fellow was the author of a young lady's pregnancy and, because the prospective papa had no money, he ordered him to give the girl a cow that she could sell to cover the cost of her confinement.

Shortly thereafter, it was revealed that the girl wasn't pregnant after all. What's more, she'd sold the cow and spent the money.

What to do?

"Well," said the magistrate, "we could give the fellow another chance."

Donald V. Hambling, Q.C., former City Solicitor for the City of Ottawa, says he was often obliged to prosecute "a most stubborn Irishman named Finnerty" for continually and flagrantly violating the city's housing-standards bylaw. Every time he appeared in court to answer a charge, Finnerty had a different lawyer in tow. He got a number of adjournments that way, saying he needed time to brief his new counsel.

One day Magistrate Glenn Strike, a very patient man, said enough was enough. He gave another trial date and said that come hell or high water, the case would be heard then.

On the appointed day, Finnerty stood alone before the bar of justice, holding in both hands a crude wooden cross about four feet high.

"Who's your counsel today, Mr. Finnerty?" the magistrate asked.

"Yer Honour, God is me counsel!"

Magistrate Strike broke into a wide grin and said to the prosecutor, "Well, Mr. Hambling, that's pretty tough competition. Would *you* like an adjournment so that you may consider retaining *outside* counsel?"

Denis Archambault, a lawyer in Prince George, British Columbia, tells about another man who stood alone before the bar of justice. He was charged with an "indictable" offence – that is, a serious charge – and was given the usual threefold choice as to how he could be tried: "You have the right to be tried by a magistrate without a jury, or a judge without a jury, or a judge and jury. How do you wish to be tried?"

The unrepresented man appeared confused. He thought for a moment, then blurted, "Trial without a judge."

The courtroom rocked with laughter and Provincial Court Judge George Stewart looked at the accused and said, "Young man, you're probably in the right place."

A New Brunswick judge, who had other interests besides the law, rarely heard cases in the afternoon. One day, as noon approached, he suggested to an out-of-town lawyer that the impaired driving case he was hearing should be concluded the next day. The lawyer objected, saying the the accused and his witnesses couldn't afford to lose another day away from work, and the judge replied:

"Well, all right, but I should tell you that no one has ever been acquitted in this court in the afternoon."

The case was continued the next day.

"Brevity is the soul of wit," goes an old saying. If so, you can't top a remark made by Mr. Justice H.Y. MacDonald of the Saskatchewan Court of Queen's Bench.

An employer was charged with seducing his employee, who later had a child. Defence counsel pleaded for leniency, saying, "He has no previous record, My Lord. He's a family man who has seven children."

"Eight," said the judge.

The late Farquhar ("Scotty") MacRae was a County Court judge in Toronto for many years. One day, he was scheduled to hear charges of assault causing bodily harm against six members of a motorcycle gang. The accused decided to plead guilty and the defence lawyers and Crown Attorney agreed on what sentences would be proper, based on the records of the accused men. As is common in such cases, they met to discuss it with the judge.

It was agreed among the lawyers that three of the defendants should get nine months and the other three should get three months, not to take effect until after Christmas. The judge thought the sentences were fair.

Judge MacRae had had a stroke and, not trusting his memory as much as he had in the past, he wrote everything down – the names of each accused and what sentence each was to receive in January.

On the day appointed for sentencing, Judge MacRae mounted the Bench and said, "Gentlemen, I've lost the minutes of settlement."

He gave everyone six months, then said: "I wish to make it clear that three of you were supposed to get sentences of nine months; you are now getting only six months. Three of you, however, were supposed to get sentences of three months; you are now getting six months.

"Now, the ones who were going to get nine months owe three months to the ones who got six months but should have got three months. You can work that out among yourselves!"

With that, the judge rose and left the courtroom.

Jack Hughes, who was the court clerk that day, says none of the men complained. "They all marched off to serve their sentences without a whimper from anyone."

Jack Hughes also remembers a day when a rookie judge heard some identification evidence from a woman witness. The man she'd seen on the night in question had white hair "exactly like that man over there," she said, pointing to a court attendant. The judge said immediately, "I'd like to have that man marked as an exhibit."

Mr. Justice Carl Stewart, of the Supreme Court of Ontario, was hearing a divorce case based on allegations of mental cruelty.

The petitioner testified that her husband swore, came home late, gambled, abused her verbally, paid no attention to her and generally made life miserable.

"Don't you have any more evidence?" His Lordship asked the woman's lawyer.

"No, My Lord," the lawyer said. "That's all the evidence I've got. I submit I've established mental cruelty."

"It sounds more like reasonable wear and tear," said the judge.

Magistrate D.B. Menzies, who presided for many years in London, Ontario, heard a woman's claim for support against her husband. The couple had lived together for only three months, then separated. The judge awarded twenty dollars a month.

"Your Worship," the woman's lawyer said, "that's not very much."

"Well," said the magistrate, "he didn't get very much."

Patrick Ryan, Q.C., of Fredericton, New Brunswick, tells about the time an R.C.M.P. officer was given a warrant for the arrest of a putative father. Judge Charlie Tweeddale, of nearby Minto, instructed the officer on how to serve the document:

"You know how they arrest a ship on a warrant in an admiralty case, don't you?"

"No, Your Honour, I don't."

"They nail the warrant to the mast. Now go and do your duty!"

An Ontario Supreme Court judge was hearing divorce cases in Guelph, one day about twenty years ago. A man giving vital information to the court was asked by his lawyer, "And when were you married?"

"Ten years ago today."

The judge looked down and said sweetly, "Happy anniversary!"

Former Alberta Chief Justice C.C. McLaurin was a cranky, impatient judge who ploughed through cases in jig time and used words as if they cost sixty dollars each. "Coin of the realm or the Order will go!" he'd say to mortgagors pleading for time in foreclosure actions. "Pay the Jane off!" he'd roar when a husband disputed the amount of alimony he was saddled with. "Get them into bed!" he'd bark to a lawyer he thought slow in presenting evidence of adultery in a divorce case.

"There is only one known instance of the Chief Justice ever taking the time to listen to counsel cite precedents," writes Jim Ross, Q.C., of Edmonton. "It occurred in Calgary and those members of the bar who were present were amazed when the Chief Justice indulged counsel by listening to quotation after quotation from volumes of law reports which stretched the length of the counsel table.

"At the conclusion of the applicant's submissions, the Chief Justice asked if that was all and, on being informed that it was, stated: 'Bullshit, costs to the respondent!' "

Compare that with the almost-gentle but effective rebuke of another Alberta judge, a member of the Court of Queen's Bench who wishes to remain anonymous.

"A long commercial trial had concluded and counsel for the defendant was addressing me," the judge writes. "He had covered every conceivable point at least four times and it was nearly time to rise for the day.

"Counsel observed me looking at my watch. He interrupted his address and said: 'My Lord, I noticed that you were looking at the time. Am I taking too long?' My response was: 'I wasn't looking at the time. I was looking at the date.' Needless to say, his address terminated within a few minutes."

A somewhat similar story comes from the Ontario Court of Appeal. One morning, in the mid-1940s, John Arnup, a leading Toronto lawyer, was ready to start his argument for the respondent in an appeal when he was told that Chief Justice R.S. Robertson wished to see him before the opening of court.

"Mr. Justice Hogg has diarrhoea this morning," the Chief Justice informed Mr. Arnup. "He would appreciate it if you would make your argument as short as possible. The court will be reconstituted after your case."

Mr. Arnup was on the horns of a dilemma: Should he risk embarrassing his client by shortening his argument, or should he risk embarrassing Mr. Justice Hogg by taking too long? He decided to be as brief as he could and made a very short argument. "I had one eye on my notebook and one eye on Mr. Justice Hogg," he said later.

Judgement was reserved and, lickety-split, the court was reconstituted. When judgement was given a few days later, it included this cryptic comment:

"We are all very much indebted for the cogent and succinct argument of Mr. Arnup."

It was an almost-moving experience.

An earlier member of the same court, Sir William Mulock, provides us with another example of terse humour. Sir William, a sharp-witted gentleman who lived to be more than one hundred and was still gracing the Ontario Court of Appeal in his mid-nineties, was walking with a fellow Justice one day when they passed an extremely attractive young woman. Both men turned for another look and Sir William sighed: "Oh, to be ninety again!"

If you like fast wit, harken to this. A Manitoba judge recently gave a man a much heftier jail term than the man had expected. They had a short conversation which went as follows:

"I'm sentencing you to a year in prison."

"Well, I'll be fucked!"

"Not for a year you won't!"

That naughty word popped up in a British Columbia bestiality case involving a man and a dog. The judge who had acquitted the man was informed by a court official that the B.C. Court of Appeal had just reversed his decision.

"It doesn't surprise me," the judge said. "They know more about fucking the dog than I do."

Mr. Justice Jimmy Cairns, of the Alberta Court of Queen's Bench and later of the Alberta Court of Appeal, once listened as a trial judge to a long recitation of infidelities by a husband. The witness described with unbecoming frankness his repeated adulteries, naming women and places in a carnal confession that over-awed the judge. At the conclusion of the testimony, Mr. Justice Cairns was heard to say, "It is very difficult to tell where the evidence ends and the boasting begins."

In a divorce case based on adultery, the petitioner's lawyer, a pompous fellow, asked his client, "What was the first thing you did when you learned of your husband's infidelity?"

"I went to see a lawyer."

"You mean you went to see me."

"Well, that's just as good," Mr. Justice Cairns interjected.

And at the opening of a murder trial in Lethbridge, about twenty-five years ago, a man asked to be excused from jury duty because, "My wife is about to conceive a baby."

"Your Honour, I think he means his wife is about to deliver a baby," the Crown Attorney observed.

"Well," said Mr. Justice Cairns, "he should be there in either event."

The late Mr. Justice Walter Kirke-Smith, of the Supreme Court of British Columbia, presided at a trial in the old Vancouver court house, in a courtroom directly below one of the rooms used by the Court of Appeal.

During the trial, a trickle of water started to run down the wall behind the judge. The flow increased until there was quite a stream. The lawyers pointed this out to Mr. Justice Kirke-Smith, who turned around and surveyed the situation, then turned back to counsel, cast his eyes toward the ceiling and exclaimed: "It must be a message from the Court of Appeal!"

Isaac Rice was a sharp-tongued Winnipeg magistrate with a flair for innovative punishments such as "house arrest" and "community work orders." It annoyed him greatly that governments and higher courts criticized his judicial innovations, and he often lamented from the Bench that no one supported his crusades for more flexible criminal justice.

One morning, in the middle of a trial at the old Rupert Street Police Station, the ceiling above the bench collapsed and Magistrate Rice was showered with plaster.

"You see!" he shouted, raising his hands towards Heaven, "I don't even get support from up there!"

The legendary Mr. Justice Harold Riley figured prominently in another case involving damage to a court house. His Lordship had two large poodles that he often brought to his office in Calgary. Court orderlies were assigned to the job of walking the dogs and of making sure they didn't get out of the office while their master was in court.

Gordon Douglas, manager of the Vancouver office of Carswell Legal Publications, was a court clerk in the Calgary Court House in the early 1960s, and one day an orderly came into court and handed him a note addressed to Mr. Justice Riley. Gord handed the note up to the judge, who read it, then interrupted the proceedings to say, "Gentlemen, you'll have to excuse me. I've just had an urgent communication from one of my colleagues."

His Lordship left the bench, then paused and said theatrically, "I suppose I really owe you gentlemen a word of explanation. I've just received a note from Mr. Justice Porter. I think I should read it to you. It says: Harold, to quote Sir Winston Churchill, 'there comes a time when every man must stand and do his duty.' Your time has arrived. Your dogs shit on my carpet. Marsh."

Mr. Justice Willard ("Bud") Estey, of the Supreme Court of Canada, also has a story about a note delivered to a judge. In the late 1930s, two members of the Supreme Court of Canada had to go to Montreal to attend a dinner. They were going to leave after court.

That afternoon one of the judges wondered who was playing against the Montreal Canadiens in the hockey game that night, and asked an usher to find out.

While court was in session, the usher brought in a note which read: "Canadiens v. Boston." By mistake, the note was handed to Sir Lyman Duff, Chief Justice of Canada. He read it, looked puzzled and said to the usher, "I've never heard of *that* case."

The stick-handling in the game the judges attended couldn't compare with the dipsy-doodle performance of the late Judge Stuart Van Male of the Provincial Court of British Columbia. One morning, in the early 1970s, Judge Van Male sentenced a man to nine months in jail – three months more than the law permitted for the kind of offence he'd committed.

Having heard of his error after the accused had left the courtroom, the judge ordered that the man be brought back before him at 1:30 p.m. that day. When the man reappeared, did the judge admit his mistake? No sirree. He saw a way out.

"I've been talking to the corrections personnel," he said, "and they tell me you were a model prisoner this morning. Now I'm going to reward you for your exemplary behaviour. Your sentence is hereby reduced to six months."

Mr. Justice Rene Foisy, of the Alberta Court of Queen's Bench, has what his colleague, Mr. Justice John McClung, calls "a priceless, horse-sense insight into the realities of life." He calls 'em as he sees 'em and he uses down-to-earth lingo, too.

In a recent prosecution under the Criminal Code, the Crown Attorney submitted that the crime had been properly proven and the accused should be convicted.

His Lordship didn't see it that way at all. Why, he said, the Alberta Poultry Act had more bearing on the case than the Criminal Code. "This whole prosecution is chicken shit," he declared, "and I'm dismissing it."

Another no-nonsense judge was Frederick Montye Morson, who served on the County Court of the County of York, in Toronto, from 1892 to 1931. "Monty," as he was known affectionately to two generations of lawyers and law students, was a wise, witty jurist who always cut straight to the heart of a matter. When he conducted Small Claims Court, he routinely decided forty cases a day.

One of those cases concerned a woman who went to law over a canary. The woman, acting on her own behalf, sued the owner of a pet store, alleging that he sold her a canary that was guaranteed to sing but didn't.

"How do you know the canary wouldn't sing?" Monty asked her.

"I beg your pardon."

He asked her the same question again and again and each time the plaintiff said, "I beg your pardon."

"Case dismissed!" Judge Morson ruled. "If you can't hear me you couldn't hear the canary!"

Just as emphatic was another Ontario judge who tossed out an indecent assault case.

"To have the court believe that this assault took place in a Ford coupe is ridiculous," he declared. "Even if the girl had been willing, there isn't enough room. I had a Ford coupe and I know!"

3

Twelve Good
and True

You never know what a jury will do.

If you have a weak case, jurors might take a liking to you, or a scunner to the other guy, and hand you the verdict. Toronto criminal lawyer Bill Murphy had a bizarre case that proves this point. If you were giving it a label, you might call it "The Case of the Man Who Had Tunnel Vision."

Back in the early '70s, Murphy defended a man who was charged with making threatening phone calls – to wit, threatening to blow up the C.B.C. building in Toronto. Murphy did extensive research into the background of the Crown's chief witness and found something that might help a great deal.

The jury trying the case liked the witness. They took everything he said as the gospel truth and, as Bill Murphy rose to cross-examine, it looked like "curtains" for the defence.

To win the case, Murphy would have to zap this witness, totally destroy his credibility. All he had going for him was that the witness had been convicted of vagrancy. No big deal, as the saying goes. That wasn't likely to turn the jury against him. But it was an unusual form of "vagrancy" the man had been convicted of, and the circumstances of the case were, to put it mildly, quite different. Murphy knew that if the judge allowed him to explore those circumstances, he might still score a victory.

"Have you ever been convicted of a criminal offence?" Murphy asked the witness.

"Yes."

"Impeding a woman, wasn't it?"

"Yes."

"What's that?" asked Judge Garth Moore, quite interested.

"Impeding a woman, Your Honour. May I proceed?"

The judge gave him the green light.

"Isn't it true," Murphy asked the star witness, "that near Uxbridge, Ontario, you dug a tunnel under an outdoor toilet and watched women relieving themselves?"

"Well, yes," gulped the witness, amazed that Murphy knew about this.

"You wore rubber boots and a plastic hat and a plastic coat and you stood there looking up at women who were going to the toilet, isn't that right, witness?" Murphy asked, cheekily.

"Y-y-yes," the man gulped again.

"And you did this for some time, until a woman happened to look down and see you, and she had you arrested. Correct?"

"That's right."

The jury, now filled with loathing, figured they couldn't believe the man's previous evidence and acquitted Murphy's client.

Former Canadian Prime Minister John Diefenbaker was a very good trial lawyer who often had his way with juries. In his first jury case, Diefenbaker defended a man charged with the attempted murder of his neighbour. The accused said he took a shot at the fellow, thinking he was a coyote foraging in the dim light of early evening.

In his charge to the jury, the trial judge suggested that the accused be convicted of the lesser offence of "wounding." The jury disregarded the suggestion and let the young lawyer's client off completely.

After the trial was over, the judge, accidentally on purpose, fell into conversation with one of the jurors. He was curious to know what had led them to acquit.

"It's the kid's first case," one of the jurors had informed his colleagues. That won a few votes.

"Yeah," said another juror, "and it's his birthday too." That did it! The Birthday Boy went "over the top."

The late Arthur Maloney, Q.C., of Toronto, one of the finest jury lawyers Canada has ever produced, loved to tell about his first jury case, which he said was his most satisfying.

His client was charged with embezzlement, and the evidence against him was so overwhelming that Maloney urged him to plead guilty and throw himself on the mercy of the court. The client wouldn't hear of it. "I've paid you a good retainer and I want you to defend the case vigorously," he told the young lawyer. "What's more, I want a jury trial."

"A jury will crucify you," Maloney warned.

"No matter! Do what I say! Give it everything you've got!" Maloney said he would, but he was far from optimistic.

The trial judge was notorious for badgering and bullying young counsel; he felt it was part of their education. Maloney was well aware of this. He prepared his case thoroughly and resolved that the nasty judge wouldn't get his goat. The judge was on Maloney's back from start to finish, interrupting him constantly and treating him like dirt, but Counsel managed to keep his cool.

Arthur told the jurors it was his first jury trial, and he noted in passing that he would never be able to make that statement again. He said everything he could in favour of his client, then sat down, heavy-hearted. He felt there was only one possible verdict – guilty. He was positive of this when the jury returned after only ten minutes of deliberation.

They found the accused not guilty. The judge exploded with anger. He called the jurors irresponsible and said their verdict was a disgrace.

An hour or so later, the foreman and several members of the jury were drinking in the beverage room of the hotel where Maloney had been staying. The foreman noticed Arthur checking out and invited him to join the group.

"Well, young fellow, how'd you like our verdict?" the foreman asked.

"I loved it," Maloney said, "but I think you were dead wrong."

"Oh, yeah, we knew it was the wrong verdict," the man said, "but we were determined to teach that old bastard a lesson for tormenting you all through the trial!"

District Court Judge Edward J. Houston, of Ottawa, who had many jury trials when he was a practising lawyer, laughs when he recalls one that he and "Jake" Dunlap appeared in about twenty years ago. The trial was in Pembroke, in the heart of the Ottawa Valley, where both lawyers had their roots. Their opponents were from a big Toronto litigation firm.

As the prospective jurors filed into the small courtroom, the Toronto lawyers grew increasingly uneasy.

"Hi, Eddie," one of the panel hailed Houston.

"How's it going, Jake?" another sang out to Dunlap.

Eight jurymen, in all, greeted the local lawyers. It's not an offence to be popular, and it sure can help.

The Toronto lawyers, who had spurned every offer of settlement, became edgy when they thought of what that friendly jury might do. Houston told Dunlap as the trial began, "They'll be down to see us tonight."

He was right. The city slickers showed up after supper and settled the case in jig time.

Another veteran Ottawa trial lawyer, Roydon Hughes, Q.C., had a jury case that's probably unique in Canada. Back in prohibition days, Hughes represented two Montreal men who were charged with transporting alcohol into Ontario. They pleaded not guilty, but the Mounties had an overwhelming case against them.

When the jurors were retiring to consider their verdict, Hughes asked that all exhibits – including numerous cans of alcohol – be sent into the jury room with them. The judge so ordered.

"The jury went in about 4:30 in the afternoon," Hughes told a recent legal gathering. "They came back at 11:30 at night and they were all laughing and cheering." No wonder – they had drunk a gallon of evidence.

By the way, the verdict was not guilty.

Occasionally in a jury case, a lawyer who's blessed with a sense of humour will "laugh the case out of court." It's a rare talent which in these "uptight" times is in danger of extinction. It involves making light of the evidence and jollying up the jury to the point where they say, in effect, "what the hell, this isn't very serious" and let the bloke off.

Toronto criminal lawyer Bill Murphy has been known to "laugh" juries into an acquitting mood. In one such case, about twenty years ago, Murphy defended a man who was charged with stealing one hundred cases of Bromo Seltzer.

The chief Crown witness was one of the top men from the company that manufactured Bromo – a "Mr. Belch." Murphy had a ball with that one. So did the jury. Murphy had them in stitches for the rest of the trial. The jury acquitted his client and the next day the headline in the Toronto *Telegram* read: "Bromo Seltzer Case Fizzles."

There's an ancient, and interesting, ritual that's followed when a jury is selected to try a criminal case. As each potential juror steps forward for consideration by the defence, the court clerk says: "Prisoner, look at the juror. Juror, look at the prisoner." In one magic moment, defence lawyer and client are supposed to know whether they want that person on the jury. If they do, the lawyer says "content." Otherwise, he says "challenge."

In a case tried at Windsor, Ontario, the court clerk, no doubt thinking of the name of the juror, announced: "Prisoner, look at the juror. Juror, look at your Peter."

The juror, it's reported, immediately looked down at his crotch.

The routine just described, with or without the downward glance, can take a fair bit of time. After all, twelve acceptable jurors do have to be found.

Toronto lawyer Rod MacGregor acted in a recent case in which his client got to meet a couple of dozen potential jurors in the time-honoured way, then saw half of them take their seats in the jury box. "Ladies and gentlemen of the jury," the accused heard the judge say, "before we hear any evidence I will now outline your duties as jurors."

When the judge had performed that important function, the accused called his lawyer over to the prisoner's dock and asked: "Who *are* those people?"

4

Witnesses

God bless witnesses!

They inject a lot of comedy into our courtrooms, brightening the proceedings with wonderfully unexpected answers that leave you grinning or chuckling or sometimes splitting your sides laughing. As any doctor will tell you, such moments of mirth are extremely good for your health.

In the interest of national well-being, I present herewith a smorgasbord of stories, collected from sea to shining sea, in which witnesses get all the best lines. They're Canadian witnesses, every last one of them, and I think we should be proud of them.

In Vancouver, Allan D. Thackray, Q.C., defended a doctor in a malpractice suit arising from the removal of a small lump from a man's groin. The plaintiff alleged that the doctor botched the job and as a result his sexual prowess, formerly of Olympic calibre, was now pretty ordinary.

At a pre-trial examination under oath, Mr. Thackray asked the plaintiff to tell him about his sexual problems.

Well, the man said, not long before the operation he was unemployed for a month and a half and he whiled away the time with a woman of his acquaintance.

"I kept tabs on the calendar just seeing how good I was, seven times a day for thirty days," the plantiff said, "and I can go before a lie detector if you want proof. A lie detector don't lie."

"Were you living with the woman?" asked the lawyer, who supplied me with a transcript of part of the examination.

"Yes."

"So you were having intercourse seven times a day?"

"For thirty days, yes."

"Did you continue to live with that lady?"

"No."

"Why not?"

"Would you live with a cheat? She was fooling around on the side!"

An elderly Edmonton couple shuffled off to divorce court. He was in his eighties, she in her late seventies. The judge granted the decree but, his curiosity getting the better of him, asked the petitioner why they'd waited so long to untie the knot.

"Because of the children," he replied. "We didn't want to embarrass them, so we waited until they were all dead."

Mr. Justice R.A.F. Montgomery, of the Court of Queen's Bench of Alberta, tells of a robbery case he tried in Edmonton in June of 1984. The accused was the customer of a very attractive twenty-year-old prostitute, who testified at the trial as a Crown witness. Defence counsel cross-examined the woman, trying to show how immoral – and presumably how unworthy of belief – she was.

"What were your weekly earnings in August of 1983?" he asked.

"Two thousand to three thousand per week."

"Of course, you would declare these earnings in your income tax return?"

"No, I did not."

"Why not?"

"Because I didn't receive any T-4 slips."

In an Ontario case, a man stole the cash box from a brothel he'd visited. His defence to a theft charge was that he merely reimbursed himself for the money he'd forked over for a very substandard performance by one of the staff. Not so, said the madam. She pointed out that he'd swiped *all* the money.

Defence counsel, who was highly respected, cross-examined the madam on how she would know how much money was in the cash box. He asked if she kept books of record and she said no.

"Come, come, Mrs. – ," he said, "you must have some system. Or do you not have any system at all?"

The madam, who was renowned for her wit as well as her beauty, rocked the court with the reply: "Mr. – you've been there so often, you know very well what the system is!"

Percy Hagel, a controversial Winnipeg lawyer, was disbarred and sent to prison for helping a murder suspect escape from custody in 1914. A few years later he talked the Law Society of Manitoba into letting him resume practice, but his prison record sometimes came back to haunt him, like the time he asked a witness where he'd been on a certain day in 1915.

"You should know," the witness answered. "You were in the next cell block!"

Montreal lawyer Gerald C. Burke reports that during a trial in Sessions Court in Montreal in the fall of 1984, the presiding judge and "a cute young female witness" who'd just been sworn in had the following conversation:

"Young lady, haven't I seen you somewhere before?"

"No, Your Lordship, I don't think you have."

"Are you sure? I really do think that we have met recently."

"I'm quite sure. I know that we have never met before."

"Please, young lady, I know that we have in fact met before. Please tell me where."

"Well, if you must know, Your Lordship, I was dancing on your table last night!"

Mr. Burke concludes his report: "The judge, red-faced, immediately recessed the court."

Judge Guy Goulard, of the Provincial Court (Family Division) in Ottawa, tells of a case he tried in which a six-foot 200-pound woman claimed that her 120-pound husband had deserted her. The husband said in a small, wimpy voice: "Your Honour, I'm not a deserter. I'm a refugee."

Rod Ferguson, Q.C., of Midland, Ontario, serves from time to time as an acting Small Claims Court judge. He recalls an occasion when he heard one dreary "judgement summons" case after another – cases involving debtors who have to explain why they have failed to pay on judgements or else go to jail for contempt of court. All the debtors except one had some sort of flimsy excuse and they promised to straighten up and fly right. The other fellow had no excuse whatever. To him the case was a big yawn.

Ferguson was frustrated, and he showed it.

"You owe the money, and you've made no attempt to make any payments," he began his sermon to the debtor. "What's more, you've said you're not even going to try to pay. How do you explain this? What's the reason?"

"I dunno," the man said. "I guess I'm just an asshole."

Judge N.G. Hewitt of the Alberta Provincial Court (Family Division) heard a child welfare case involving a likeable woman whose first name was Mary. She had lost all of her other children to the Children's Aid Society and had lived "common law" with a succession of men.

Mary told the court she should be allowed to keep her last child because she'd finally found a man who was right for her. She said she and the man were going to settle down and the home would be a proper one for the child.

Judge Hewitt had heard all the evidence and he saw things differently. He was going to have to take the last child from her, and in pronouncing his judgement, he began softly with these words:

"Mary, I like you. . ."

"Well, you're too late!" Mary said crisply.

As Richard Nixon would say, I want to make one thing perfectly clear: There's nothing funny about the act of rape. However, many humorous things are said at rape trials, usually unintentionally.

Former Ontario Chief Justice G.A. Gale agrees, and he offers this recollection:

"On one occasion in Toronto I was presiding at a rather unspectacular rape trial when a witness, Mrs. Schroeder, was called. She was brought in the southeast door of Courtroom 2 in City Hall in a dreadful condition. Indeed, the female attendant finally had to half-carry her to the witness box. She shook so badly that the registrar could not administer the oath.

"I finally tried to lend a hand by endeavouring to calm her down and explain exactly what her involvement was. Her reply was to this effect: 'Judge, I have never had such a terrible experience in my life. I am absolutely petrified. I don't want anything to do with a court, now or ever in the future. In fact, I'm going to stop watching Perry Mason on T.V.' "

In Manitoba, a complainant in a rape case testified that she'd tarried for some time in a tavern and, after sharing a few brews with the accused, who'd left his table to join her, she said so long and started for home. The man followed her, she said, then grabbed her, threw her to the ground and started having his way with her.

"Did you tell him to stop?" the prosecutor asked.

"I did."

"Why?"

"Because he was crushing my cigarettes!"

In another rape case, in Peterborough, Ontario, defence counsel, in cross-examining the complainant, suggested that the woman had been familiar with the accused on previous occasions.

"You went with him all last summer, didn't you?"

"Yes."

"Well, I suggest that you had intercourse with him many times last summer."

"Oh, yes," came the surprise reply, "it was nothing but rape, rape, rape all summer long!"

There's also nothing funny about murder, but humour can erupt in such cases too. The late Arthur Maloney, Q.C., loved to tell about an Ontario murder trial where a policeman testified: "When I arrived, the victim was still alive and he said . . ."

"Hold it! Don't say anything more!" the judge warned. "I'll have to determine whether your evidence is admissible."

A word of explanation. Quite properly, hearsay evidence may not be given in court; it's dangerous and unfair to allow it. Technically, what the deceased said to the policeman is hearsay; the deceased isn't available to affirm or deny what he's alleged to have said.

But rules are made to be broken, and there are exceptions to the ban on hearsay evidence. For centuries, the courts have said that a "dying declaration," though hearsay, may be given in evidence. It's presumed that no one who's about to meet his Maker would dare die with a lie on his lips. This is one hell of a presumption because many people wouldn't hesitate to exit lying, but that's the law.

As is usual in such cases, the judge told the jury to retire to their room and he started to conduct a "voir dire" – a trial within a trial – to determine whether they should be permitted to hear what the deceased said to the policeman. That would depend on whether the statement *was* a dying declaration, and that, in turn, hinged on whether the man *knew* he was dying when he said what he said.

For several hours, the lawyers for the Crown and the defence argued subtle legal points. The Crown, of course, contended that the statement was a genuine, honest-to-God dying declaration and should be admitted into evidence. The defence argued that the deceased didn't know he was dying when he spoke and so his utterance should be kept out of the record.

The judge said it was a toughie and he wanted to study some precedents and think about things overnight. In the morning, he announced that he had decided that the statement was admissible. The policeman returned to the stand.

"Now, officer," the Crown Attorney said, "yesterday you were about to tell us what the deceased said when you arrived on the scene. Please tell His Lordship and the jury what he said."

"Well, he just said 'Ugh!' and died."

Several years ago, Bob McGee, Deputy Crown Attorney of Metropolitan Toronto, prosecuted a case in which a gangster was charged with murdering a rival mobster and his girlfriend. It was a difficult case which lasted several weeks and it consisted mainly of wire-tap evidence that was largely circumstantial.

Bob, who earned the flattering nickname of "Fair Trial McGee," was winding up a long cross-examination of the accused when he said something he immediately wished he hadn't:

"I suggest to you that when you swear that you didn't murder these people, you sir, are a liar!"

The accused glared at the prosecutor, then barked: "And I suggest that you, sir, are full of shit!"

That was bad enough, but then the accused's common-law wife applauded and shouted, "Good for you, dear!"

What's more, the judge started to laugh, then, mercifully, gained control of himself.

Bob sat down, chagrined. The spectators started to laugh and, after a moment or two, so did McGee. The judge called a brief recess to give everyone a chance to stop giggling.

John "Jake" Dunlap loves to tell stories of the Ottawa Valley, where he was born and raised. The Valley abounds with eccentric characters, and one of his favourites was "Straight Back" Maloney, a man of few words.

"Straight Back" appeared as a witness in an action brought by a Valley farmer against the Canadian Pacific Railroad. A train hit a number of the farmer's pigs and the farmer sued for the price of the animals. The witness told everything he knew about the matter.

"Now, Mr. Maloney, what was the first thing you saw?" he was asked.

"The first thing I seed was the train comin' down the track."

"What was the second thing you saw?"

"The second thing I seed was the pigs comin' out of the alfalfa."

"What was the next thing you saw?"

"The next thing I seed was the alfalfa comin' out of the pigs."

Tom Hubbard, a long-time court reporter and former Chief of the Reporting Branch of the Canadian Senate, recalls a divorce case in which he recorded the evidence. (Before 1968, Quebecers who wished a divorce had to present evidence to a Senate committee and, if they succeeded, the bonds of matrimony were severed by an Act of Parliament.)

A Quebec man sought a divorce from his wife, based on the only ground available – adultery. To save money, he skipped the usual routine of hiring a private detective and brought along his brother to air the dirty linen.

The witness testified that from a vantage point on a balcony he had looked into a window and seen his sister-in-law and the co-respondent making love on a bed.

"You mean to say you actually saw the intercourse take place?" the petitioner's solicitor asked.

The witness replied: "I did not see de ting go into de ting, but I saw his arse go 'hip, hip, horray!' "

In an indecent-exposure – or, as the police might say, "flag-waving" – case, well-known Edmonton lawyer Neil D. MacLean, Q.C., was trying to destroy the evidence of the complainant, who insisted that she was shocked by what she had seen.

On direct examination, the Crown Attorney had asked her what the accused had done and she had replied, "He opened his pants and showed me his penis."

MacLean's cross-examination was getting nowhere, but then he had an inspiration. "Tell me," he said, "how big was his penis?"

"Oh," she replied, "about average."

In a similar vein, a Winnipeg policeman was testifying for the Crown in a criminal case and the Crown Attorney asked him, "Did you use profanity when you spoke to the accused?"

"No, sir!" he replied, emphatically.

"Witness, are you sure that you never called the accused a filthy name?"

"I'm positive, sir. I was brought up never to use unclean language."

When he returned to his seat and was passing the Crown Attorney, the officer asked him in a "stage whisper" that everyone could hear, "Why the fuck did you ask me those questions?"

In another Manitoba case, we have this delightful exchange:

Q. Why did you hit her?
A. First she called me a bitch. Then she called me a whore. And then she called me a dirty name, so I hit her.

And speaking of dirty names, we have this refrain from a Vancouver matrimonial case:

Q. You've heard your wife's evidence about name-calling?
A. Yes.
Q. Did you ever, as she says, call her Mrs. Asshole?
A. I never called her Mrs.

Here's another "short snapper," from an Alberta annulment case:

Q. And was the marriage consummated?
A. Not while I was there.

In an Ontario case, a very wealthy man sued his wife for divorce on the ground of her adultery. Here's part of the cross-examination of the wife by her husband's lawyer:

Q. Have you been to bed with the butler?
A. Yes.
Q. Have you been to bed with the gardener?
A. Yes.
Q. Have you been to bed with your counsel?

Her counsel leaped to his feet, waving his arms and protesting vehemently. He sighed when he heard the rest:

A. No.
Q. Why not?
A. Because he hasn't asked me.

Heather Griffiths, an Ottawa law student, tells of a case of a man charged with having sexual relations with a girl who was under the age of consent. The chief Crown witness had glanced over a hedge and had seen the couple lying on the ground in a compromising position. The cross-examining lawyer was trying to establish that things weren't necessarily what they appeared to be.

"Now, witness," he began, "when you were a young man, and courting a young lady, did you ever sit with her under a hedge on a summer's evening?"

"Yes, sir."

"And did you ever put your arm around her and maybe even find yourself lying prone with her on the ground?"

"Yes, sir."

"And someone passing by might well have jumped to the conclusion that you were engaging in sexual intercourse with the lady, mightn't they?"

"Yes, sir – and they'd have been right, too!"

The late Henry Bull, Q.C., was a top Crown Attorney in Toronto in the 1950s and '60s. During the Second World War, he was an Army officer and his duties included prosecuting servicemen.

Henry liked to tell about a buggery case he prosecuted in the Army. His chief witness testified as to the investigative work he and his men had done, then Henry asked, "What did you do then, Sergeant?"

"We buggered off," the man replied.

Judge Seamus O'Regan of the Provincial Court of Newfoundland was present in court in St. John's when "one of the town drunks" was convicted of three offences under the Intoxicated Persons Act. The judge fined the man fifty dollars on each count "or, in default, eight days."

The accused looked innocently at the judge and said, "If it's all the same to you, Your Honour, I'll take the hundred and fifty."

Victoria is a small community very near Carbonear, Newfoundland. The people there are noted for their wit and talent in making "moonshine."

One of the townsfolk was hauled into court, charged with the illegal manufacturing of spirits. The prosecutor asked a reluctant Crown witness from Victoria to name the person responsible for making the "moonshine" in Victoria.

Pensively, the witness looked at the prosecutor and said, "I don't rightly know, sir, but I'd guess it's the same fellow that makes the sun shine in Carbonear."

Mr. Justice Pierre Michaud, of the Superior Court of Quebec, tells the story of a judge who heard a case in Joliette, Quebec. The judge was gung-ho about decorum.

The plaintiff, a farmer, went into the witness box shortly after court started at 9:30 a.m. He wore old pants, a torn shirt and dirty boots. Before he was sworn, the judge addressed him:

"You knew you were coming here today, didn't you?"

"Yes."

"And you have clothes other than those you're wearing this morning, haven't you?"

"Yes, sir."

"Do you have a shirt and tie and a suit?"

"Yes."

"Why didn't you wear them to appear before the court?"

"Well, My Lord, I'll tell you. When I got up this morning at 5:30 a.m., I dressed like I am now and I went to milk the cows. Then at 6:30 I went to church and I received Communion. When I got back home, I thought about changing to come here, but then I told myself, 'Well, if the way I am dressed is good enough for God, it should be good enough for them.' "

The judge reddened and said: "Please proceed."

Federal Prosecutor Rod Flaherty of Toronto recalls a big tax fraud case he prosecuted a few years ago in Niagara Falls. The accused, an Ontario man who wheeled and dealed on both sides of the Canada-U.S. border, applied to be released on bail. Flaherty opposed the application at a bail hearing, saying that he feared the man would skip across the line and never be seen again.

"I've been here for a long time and I haven't tried to leave the country," the accused told the judge. "Why, I received information weeks ago that I was going to be charged but I stayed put. Honest, I'm ready to face the music."

"You say you received information that you were going to be charged with tax fraud?" Flaherty asked, wondering how this could be known.

"Yeah, I did."

"Tell me, how did you receive that information?"

"With a stout heart and a firm belief in my innocence!"

It's amazing how some witnesses can misinterpret the simplest questions, and get laughs in the process. C.M. Rosenblum, Q.C., of Sydney, Nova Scotia, supplies two dandy examples:

"On being arraigned before Provincial Judge John F. MacDonald on a motor vehicle charge," Mr. Rosenblum writes: "An old farmer from East Bay was asked how far he went in school and he replied: 'About three miles, Your Honour.' "

A man from the Sydney suburb of Whitney Pier appeared before the same judge, who asked him what his religion was.

"Protestant," he replied.

"What branch?"

"Whitney Pier, Your Honour."

Moving from the sublime to the ridiculous, pity the poor Manitoba witness who had to face this onslaught:

Q. Did you see whether or not your brother threw a beer bottle at Mr. Holden's car?
A. There was no beer in the car, so how could he throw one at him?
Q. So if Mr. Holden says that, he is incorrect?
A. Yes.

So far, so good. Testifying ain't hard, is it?

But wait! The judge wants to say something. We'd better listen real close:

Q. Is your reason for saying that you didn't see your brother do such a thing because it was your belief that there was no beer in the car? Or are you saying you know he actually didn't throw it? If he somehow miraculously had some passed to him through the window from another passing car, or had it concealed in his jacket and you didn't know about it, would you still say that it didn't happen that he threw beer, or did you simply know that when you got into the car half an hour before that, or whenever it was you got in, that there was no beer in the car? Whether you saw it or you didn't see it, he didn't throw any beer because you know there was no beer. The only reason for you saying that he didn't throw beer was because you believed there was no beer in the car to throw. Or can you actually say you had your brother under observation enough at the time to be able to say, even if there was a whole caseful of beer in the car at the back, he didn't throw one out? Which is it?
A. Huh?

As Art Linkletter always professed, kids say the darnedest things. In or out of court, they can stop you in your tracks. They're often a lot more knowledgeable than you think, too.

Sandra Spicer, a court reporter in Grande Prairie, Alberta, captured the testimony of a ten-year-old boy who was examined by defence counsel:

Q. How far were you from the door?
A. Ten decimeters.
Q. Ahhhhhhhh.
CROWN ATTORNEY: Ahhhhhhhh.
COURT: Ahhhhhhhhh . . . Could you point out how far?

A. From me to you.

DEFENCE COUNSEL: Thank you, sir. Darn kids today!

Halifax lawyer Donald A. Kerr, Q.C., has a wonderful story about a child witness. He tells it so well that I'm not going to touch a word of it:

"The 'unnecessary question' has caused more misery for cross-examiners than all other aspects of trial work taken together. The admonition to leave well enough alone is drummed into us at law school, and during practice, but somehow we cannot resist that final daring thrust which, good easy men, we believe will surely seal the issue – but which often brings disaster instead.

"One shining example, never to be forgotten, does more than all the lectures. The great Henry P. MacKeen, Q.C., told this one on himself, and, having learned courtroom tactics at his knee, I have never forgotten it.

"For insurers, he was defending a personal injury case involving allegedly severe leg damage to a twelve-year-old boy. Under cross-examination, the lad readily admitted that he continued his Boy Scout activities and went to summer camp. Like a bolt from the blue, he also volunteered that he played on his school's hockey team. Marvellous!

" 'And did your team do well?' probed H.P.

" 'Yes, sir, we won the championship this year,' said the boy. Even better!

"Then came the final, and fatal, question.

" 'And did you score many goals?'

" 'Oh, no, sir, I have to play goalie. I can't skate because of my bad leg!' "

An Ontario judge interviewed a lad of about ten in his chambers. The boy was the subject of a custody case and the judge wanted to chat with him privately and learn what his thoughts were on the matter.

"I've got a boy about the same age as you," His Honour said, trying to make the young fellow feel at ease. He showed him a picture of his son.

The boy glanced at it and exclaimed, "Hey, that's the kid who beat me up in the schoolyard!"

An outstanding Saskatchewan lawyer, N. Ross Craig, K.C., appeared for the defendant in a damage action heard in Regina early in the century. The plaintiff, a young farm boy, alleged he'd been kicked by the defendant's horse. One of the boy's witnesses, another lad, came to court with his father on a cold, snowy morning. The two had travelled by horse-sled from their farm near Moose Jaw. The boy was there to testify.

When he was called to the witness box, the boy was sworn to "tell the truth, the whole truth and nothing but the truth." He gave strong evidence in favour of his friend, the plaintiff, and Craig cross-examined him carefully and at great length. The youngster was an excellent witness. It was obvious that he couldn't be shaken in his testimony.

Finally, as a last resort, Craig said intimidatingly, "I suppose when you and your father travelled to Regina this morning, the two of you talked about the case?"

"Yes, sir."

"I see, I see," said the lawyer, encouraged by the answer. "And did your father tell you what to say in court?"

"Yes, sir, he did."

"Well, let's have it!" Craig said triumphantly. "Tell us what your father told you to say!"

"He told me to tell the truth," the lad shot back.

Before he can testify a witness must swear to tell the truth. As one judge said: "The person who takes an oath impliedly professes that he or she has a consciousness of the duty to speak the truth and has a realization of the consequences of and punishment for wilfully making a false assertion."

The law doesn't generally put any reliance on evidence which isn't sworn to, and a court has no inherent power to receive unsworn testimony. So in some cases – especially that of children – it must be established that the potential witness understands that he can, in some way, be punished for not telling the truth.

One lad, a lawyer's son, showed that he knew the score.

"What would happen if you told a lie?" he was asked.

"Well, that would be perjury," he said matter of factly.

An eleven-year-old boy who had been injured in an accident was being interviewed by Mr. Justice D.F. O'Leary of the Supreme Court of Ontario to see if he was competent to be sworn in as a witness.

Court reporter Bob Silk gives us the dialogue:

Q. Do you know what will happen if you don't tell the truth?
A. Yes.
Q. What will happen?
A. I will be punished.
Q. Who will punish you?

A. The Lord. (Pointing at His Lordship) Not you . . . (Pointing up) . . . The other one.

Though slight of build, E.K. Williams, Chief Justice of the Court of Queen's Bench, was a towering figure on the Manitoba legal scene for many years. Stern, correct, impeccable in dress and expression, he was the personification of a judge.

One day, in the marble grandeur of Winnipeg's Queen's Bench courtroom #1, a criminal case was being tried before Chief Justice Williams and a jury. Defence counsel sought to introduce the evidence of a small boy. To determine the boy's eligibility to be sworn as a witness, the Chief Justice tested him on his knowledge of the significance of an oath.

"Now, then, young man," His Lordship said in stentorian tones. "Do you attend church or Sunday school?"

"No, sir," replied the child, barely visible above the marble witness box.

"Well, then, do your parents have a Bible in the house?"

"No, sir."

"Do you know who God is?"

"I don't think so, sir."

"Do you mean you don't know who created the universe?"

After a long pause, the boy asked, hesitantly, "You?"

A ten-year-old boy was in court in Toronto. The Crown Attorney was quizzing him to see how much, if anything, he knew about the nature of an oath.

"What do you think God would do to you if you didn't tell the truth?" the lawyer asked.

"Send me to my room," the lad replied.

"Swear him in," said the judge.

In Manitoba, a nine-year-old boy was called as a witness in court.

"Now, Bobby," said the judge, "if we let you swear on the Bible that you will tell the truth, the whole truth and nothing but the truth, and then you tell a lie, do you know what would happen to you?"

"Yes, sir," the boy answered. "I'd be kicked out of Cubs."

"Let the witness be sworn," instructed the judge.

Another Manitoba youngster needed a bit more seasoning. In his case, the dialogue went like this:

Q. Do you know what perjury is? You're nodding yes. What is it?

A. Perjury is just –

Q. Pardon?
A. It's just the same like –
Q. Speak up so I can hear you.
A. Like –
Q. What? Speak up, what is it?
A. Making –
Q. Have you got a speech defect or something, son?
A. No.
Q. All right, what is perjury then?
A. It's just the same as making sex, a different type of sex.
Q. I can't hear you.
A. Making sex that's different.
Q. Making sex, is that what you said?
A. Different.
The Court: This fellow doesn't understand the nature of an oath.

And while we're on the subject of kids, Robert D. McIntyre, Q.C., of Brampton, Ontario, "learned" some things about himself that he didn't know – thanks to his seven-year-old son. The McIntyre family visited friends who had a video tape machine. Rising for breakfast one morning, Mom and Dad discovered that an hour or so earlier their host had "interviewed" their boy on the video machine, as follows:

Q. What does your father do?
A. He's a lawyer.
Q. What does a lawyer do?
A. He helps people.
Q. How does he help people?
A. Well, if a person comes from Japan or China and they had a car and it broke down, he'd help them.
Q. How?
A. He'd give them a wrench!
Q. What type of law does your father practise?
A. He's a real estate lawyer.
Q. What does a real estate lawyer do?
A. Well, if a person goes to sell his house, he helps him put up the sign on the lawn!

Out of the mouths of babes . . .

5

Oh, Those Witty Lawyers!

*Wit is the rarest quality to be met with
among people of education.*

– WILLIAM HAZLITT

Now just a darn minute, Mr. Hazlitt. I'll have you know that we lawyers take umbrage at that remark. If you think of *us* that way, it's a bum rap.

Lawyers go to school almost as long as brain surgeons, and they're a lot funnier, too. Generally speaking, lawyers are generally speaking. And when they're speaking, why, they often say very witty things. They really do.

You obviously aren't aware of this, Mr. Hazlitt, or you would have excluded us from your cruddy comment. We're human, you know. We have feelings, like anyone else. We bleed, like anyone else.

A bunch of us got together recently, by mail, by telephone and in person, and it didn't take us long to build a strong case against you. We want you to hear that case – an all-Canadian case – and we hope that when the evidence is in you'll be man enough to eat your words.

Exhibit A is John "Jake" Dunlap.

Jake, a former professional football player, practised law in Ottawa for thirty years. These days he's Agent-General for the Province of Ontario in New York. One day, in about 1960, he represented an Ottawa woman who was found to be a prostitute. He convinced Magistrate Glen Strike that a fine, rather than imprisonment, was in order.

Magistrate Strike noted that the woman had practised her profession in a big way, and so he fined her in a big way – five hundred dollars and costs. He asked Dunlap if his client wished some time to raise the money.

Dunlap replied, "Yes, Your Worship. Could she have thirty nights to pay?"

The late Senator J.W. deB. Farris, Q.C., of Vancouver, was one of Canada's foremost trial lawyers. The Honourable N.T. Nemetz, Chief Justice of British Columbia, assisted Mr. Farris in many trials when he was at the bar, and sends this story of his former mentor:

"Before a judge and jury, the plaintiff owner of a burned-out store was suing the insurance company which had refused to pay on a fire claim. The Senator was counsel for the insurance company.

"Towards the end of the plaintiff's case, the plaintiff's counsel entered exhibits.

" 'The first,' he said, 'is a picture of the store before the fire. The second is a picture taken during the fire. And the third is a picture of the store after the fire.'

"The judge, turning to the Senator, asked, 'And do you have pictures to enter as exhibits?'

" 'No,' said Farris, 'we didn't know there was going to be a fire.' "

Winnipeg lawyer Manly Rusen is a lively, witty fellow. He's in demand as a master of ceremonies and his quips are often quoted by lawyers, judges and court officials.

One day Manly went to the Court House in Winnipeg to discuss a point of legal procedure with the Referee of the Court of Queen's Bench.

"I'd like to see the Referee," he told the court clerk.

"He's not here," said the clerk.

"Then let me talk to the head linesman," Manly shot back.

Manly's father, I.D. Rusen, was a fast-witted lawyer, too. Many years ago, when a buck went a long way, the elder Rusen met Winnipeg lawyer R.D. Guy, Jr., on the street shortly before they were to lock horns in the trial of a civil case.

They got talking about the case.

"My client will settle for fifty dollars, but not a cent more," said Mr. Guy.

"Fifty dollars!" I.D. exploded. "You think I'm fool enough – "

Guy started walking away.

" – not to take it?"

Patrick Ryan, Q.C., of Fredericton, New Brunswick, tells a wonderful story about a lawyer who was witty even when deathly ill. The nurse in the story is Pat's wife, Anne:

"In 1955, Cyrus Inches, Q.C., one of the most renowned lawyers in New Brunswick during the first half of this twentieth century, lay dying in hospital in Saint John. He had just come through an operation which required that he stay motionless in bed and, more importantly, that he remain on his side.

"His special-duty nurse, Anne B. Ryan, R.N., left the hospital room to fetch a prescribed medication for the aging lawyer. She returned to find that he had turned onto his other side. She admonished Mr. Inches for not lying on his side.

"He opened his eyes and said, 'My dear young lady, I'm a lawyer and I'm used to lying on both sides.' "

John N. Conroy, Q.C., of Saskatoon, ninety-one years young, is a retired lawyer who practised for over fifty years in North Battleford, Saskatchewan. A colourful, legendary figure in legal circles, Mr. Conroy could always be counted on to say something humorous, in person or in print. Once, representing a client who had allegedly sold an impotent bull, he held up the proceedings for some time by insisting that his opponent supply particulars which would enable him to assess his client's position – such information as the kind of surroundings provided for the bull's romantic intervals, the kind of food served to the bull and the kind of music played for him.

Another time, after skirmishing with a cranky judge, he was asked by His Honour: "Mr. Conroy, are you trying to show your contempt for this court?"

"No," he replied, "I'm trying to conceal it."

Toronto lawyer Eddie Horkins could be pretty cheeky on occasion. In a case in the Supreme Court of Ontario in the late '50s, Horkins put his client in the box, asked him his name and address and a couple of other questions and then the judge, a "take-charge guy" if ever there was one, completely commandeered the witness.

His Lordship, as was his wont, asked the man a zillion questions, and then turned to Horkins and said, "You can take over now, Mr. Horkins."

Eddie pretended not to hear him.

"You can take over now, Mr. Horkins," the judge repeated, much louder than before.

Eddie, pretending to be engrossed in his notes, ignored the judge again.

"Mr. Horkins!" the judge nearly shouted. "You can take over now."

"Oh, I'm sorry, My Lord," said Eddie. "Are you calling your next witness?"

Another Toronto lawyer had the same situation in "Police Court" in the 1930s. He handled it as follows:

"I don't mind you questioning my witness, Your Worship, but I certainly hope you don't lose the case for me."

Sometimes, flattery won't get you anywhere. Magistrate Billy McInnes of Vancouver was completing his first year on the Bench when he convicted a burglar and asked his counsel, Tom Hurley, if he had anything to say before sentence was passed.

Hurley had a tough row to hoe. His client had thirty convictions and there wasn't any evidence before the court that might help him even a teensy bit. What could the lawyer say? An idea flashed through his mind.

"Your Worship," he began, "it is just a year ago today that we were first blessed by your presence on the Bench."

A nice start. Hurley warmed to the subject. For several minutes, he extolled the virtues that had distinguished the magistrate's first year of service – especially that of compassion – and concluded by asking for a large chunk of that compassion on behalf of his client.

Magistrate McInnes replied: "From the bottom of my heart, I thank you, Mr. Hurley. I shall always cherish your compliments. But the sentence for your client will still be two years."

"In that event, Your Worship," Hurley said, "I withdraw my remarks *in toto.*"

A young lawyer was arguing his first case before the Newfoundland Court of Appeal. He expounded his position at great length, and in great detail, citing elementary principles of law.

One of the judges interrupted counsel and suggested that he get to the substance of his appeal, adding, "We're not complete idiots, you know."

"I'm sorry, My Lord," the lawyer replied, "I didn't realize that."

District Court Judge Martin Morrissey, of Brampton, Ontario, recalls a case in London, Ontario, in which a woman pleaded guilty to a charge of living off the avails of prostitution. Evidence disclosed that the accused had pressed several Indian girls into service as prostitutes, and had made a potful of money as a result.

When he heard the facts, Magistrate D.B. Menzies was horrified. "My, my, how long has this been going on?" he asked.

"Since 1492," defence counsel Jim Donahue replied.

In another case in London, a witness admitted consuming sixteen draft beers, a twelve-ounce bottle of whiskey, a twenty-five-ounce bottle of whiskey and twelve to sixteen bottles of beer, all in the course of one day. Not only that, but he denied being drunk.

My thanks to court reporter Gail McGilvray for the following:

DEFENCE COUNSEL: What is your definition of being drunk? If you can get off the floor and have one more pint, is that sober to you?

A. Well, I could have went to work that morning and my boss wouldn't have knew I was drunk.

DEFENCE COUNSEL: Do you work at the Canadian National Institute for the Blind, by any chance?

As the late Freddie Malone would say, that fellow was definitely "in the grip of the grape."

Mr. Malone, an entertaining Toronto lawyer who served twenty-nine years in the Crown Attorney's office and about fifteen more for the defence, often used that phrase. Indeed, as he'd be the first to admit, it sometimes described his own condition.

One morning, after a night of imbibing, Malone showed up half an hour late for his Crown Attorney duties. Magistrate "Gus" Thoburn had started court without him.

"Mr. Malone," he said, "we've taken the drunk cases. There aren't any more drunks to deal with."

To which Freddie replied, "Would you like to take a little bet on that, Your Worship?"

A few more stories from the Toronto magistrates' courts: About twenty years ago, an accused man appeared in court bare-chested one day. Crown Attorney Rod Cormack took one look at him and said to Magistrate Joseph Addison:

"Your Worship, it's obvious that the accused has retained counsel."

On another occasion, lawyer Tommy Horkins represented a man whose face was bleeding and bruised.

"Mr. Horkins," the magistrate said, "what happened to your client?"

Tommy replied:

"He gave a voluntary confession, Your Worship."

Toronto criminal lawyer David Cole was giving his address to a man who wanted to write him a letter. Here's how he expressed his postal code: "Murder Five Rape, One Buggery Six."

Mr. Justice John Arnup, of the Ontario Court of Appeal, tells the story of two Toronto lawyers who had a running feud for years. One lawyer wrote a scurrilous letter to the other and the recipient, thinking of what he'd like to do with it, penned this response: "Your letter is before me and shortly will be behind me."

Chief Justice Allan McEachern, of the Supreme Court of British Columbia, tells about a B.C. man who left his entire estate – a large one – to a religious sect. The deceased's family challenged the will, saying the testator didn't have all his marbles when he made it.

"Why shouldn't a man who has worked all his life be allowed to do what he wants with his estate?" asked Vancouver lawyer Wilf Heffernan, discussing the case with colleagues. "He was as sane as any of us. Look at the will, it's perfectly sensible. He's done what he wanted to do, and he hadn't seen any of these children for many years."

"Well, what evidence does the family have?" asked a doubtful listener.

"The only thing they have to go on," Heffernan replied, "is that the testator lived in a tree for the last three years of his life and he never came down once."

Chief Justice McEachern also recalls "the height of insolence" he reached years ago when a colleague took ill and was hospitalized. McEachern wrote to him and said: "The partners of my law firm authorize me to wish you a complete and speedy recovery. The vote was 8 to 7 with three abstentions."

Vancouver lawyer Rolf Weddigen once issued a statement of claim on behalf of the insurers of Her Majesty's post office trucks. He issued the document in Her Majesty's name and the first paragraph thereof read:

"The plaintiff is a married woman who lives at Buckingham Palace in the City of London, England, where she carries on the business of a Sovereign."

Several years ago, in the Ontario Court of Appeal, a lawyer was arguing the case of a man who'd been convicted of selling obscene objects. His defence was that the objects were not obscene.

The objects in question were in court for the judges to examine. One of the judges held up a large dildo and asked the lawyer: "Are you seriously contending that this object is not obscene?"

"My Lord," the lawyer said, "It is not obscene. It's a replica of part of the human body. The human body can't be obscene."

And so it went, one suggestion after another being brushed aside by the lawyer, who insisted that nothing that had been brought into court was in fact obscene. Finally, in exasperation, one of the judges said, "Mr.–, what would you say if a couple came in here right now, naked, and fornicated on the counsel table? Wouldn't that be obscene?"

"No, My Lord, that would be contempt of court."

The late Mr. Justice James Maurice King, of the Supreme Court of Ontario, was a tough judge to get a divorce from. He was a strict Catholic, rigidly opposed to divorce, and the person seeking a decree had to prove his or her case to the hilt.

Judge Emerson Perkins, of Chatham, Ontario, recalls the time in the early 1950s when Mr. Justice King came to Chatham on circuit for the first time:

"One of the lawyers had brought an uncontested action which involved evidence of a party in a large home attended by the plaintiff husband and the defendant wife. The husband had consumed more than sufficient spirits and had gone to sleep in a room on the third floor of the home.

"About four a.m. he awoke and started downstairs. On the second floor he observed his wife and another man sitting up in bed, in the nude, smoking cigarettes. The husband rushed out of the house in high dudgeon and commenced a divorce action.

"At the end of the evidence, Mr. Justice King said that he had heard a great deal of evidence of smoking, but none of adultery, and dismissed the action."

That evening, the Kent County Law Association held a dinner in honour of the visiting judge and a local lawyer, W.B. Beardall, Q.C., gave a speech of welcome. In the course of his address, which is regarded as a classic, Mr. Beardall traced the judge's career and then informed His Lordship that in Kent County "we always smoke *afterwards*, never before."

(Other Ontario cities have claimed this story as their own, but Judge Perkins says he was sitting beside Mr. Beardall when he made his speech and there can be no doubt that the honours go to Chatham.)

William Parker Fillmore, Q.C., the legendary Winnipeg wit, was trying to cross-examine a talkative witness who persisted in starting his answers before the lawyer could finish his questions. The judge instructed the man to wait until he'd heard a question before launching into his reply. Fillmore started to ask another question and the witness jumped the gun again.

"Why did you do that?" Fillmore asked.

"Well, I knew what you were going to say."

"All right," Fillmore replied, "go ahead and answer the next question."

Fillmore once acted for a man who'd spent some time in a mental institution and was later released. While he was in the institution, another person was appointed, by court order, to handle his business affairs. The former patient had a certificate, signed by a psychiatrist, stating that he was of sound mind, and he instructed Fillmore to seek a court order revoking the earlier order, so that he could once more manage his own affairs.

Chief Justice E.K. Williams, of the Manitoba Court of Queen's Bench, presided at a hearing in which Fillmore, in effect, had to convince the court that his client was indeed of sound mind. The client testified and it soon became painfully apparent that, though it was safe for him to be at large, he wouldn't be able to look after business matters. The Chief Justice said he couldn't make the order that had been requested.

Fillmore, tongue in cheek, observed, "I don't see why not, My Lord. After all, he's got his certificate. Where's *yours?*"

At least when speaking to the judge Mr. Fillmore used English. Many years ago, Wilfred Judson, who later served on the Supreme Court of Ontario and the Supreme Court of Canada, was arguing a case before a judge who criticized him for the way he pronounced a certain Latin maxim. Judson, a former Latin teacher, cooled him out. He delivered the rest of his argument in Latin.

The late Joseph Sedgwick, Q.C., of Toronto, was for many years one of the most outstanding counsel in Canada. He was also a very witty man, in and out of court.

In the early years of World War II, he did several jobs for the Finnish people at the request of Kingsley Graham, a lawyer who was Finnish consul in Toronto. Towards the end of the war, Graham met Sedgwick on a train going to Ottawa. He said the Finnish government was very grateful to Joe for what he'd done and wanted to present him with one of the country's decorations.

"Well, what do you have?" Sedgwick asked.

Graham thought for a moment, then said, "Our highest award is the Order of Chastity."

"Do you have one, fourth class?" Joe inquired.

Joe Sedgwick was counsel in a combines case that dragged on sixty-four days, much of it spent in the dreary reading-into-the-record of hundreds of documents. One day Joe dozed off for a while and when he came to he said to the lawyer next to him, "This is the dullest case I've ever been in. Even my self-winding wrist-watch has stopped!"

Mr. Justice John Arnup, of the Ontario Court of Appeal, is a giant in the profession but quite small physically. When he was still at the bar, he was once pitted against a tall, heavy-set lawyer who commented, "Isn't it too bad they abolished trial by battle?"

Speaking of small, Jane P. Cartwright, a lawyer in Kelowna, British Columbia, reports that one day recently she and a colleague, Bob Levin, sat at the back of Family Court waiting for their cases to be heard. Both cases involved consent orders, which could be dealt with very quickly. Bob is five-foot-four and Jane is five-two.

The court clerk announced: "Your Honour, we have just two short matters left."

"That's us, Your Honour," cracked Levin.

During argument in Provincial Court, Crown Attorney Ken Rae, Q.C., of Owen Sound, Ontario, took a verbal swipe at his opponent:

"Your Honour, my friend's ignorance of the law surprises me."

"Surely you can rephrase that," said the judge.

"All right," Rae replied. "My friend's ignorance of the law doesn't surprise me."

Rae prosecuted a case in Kitchener, Ontario, about fifteen years ago, in which there were five or six accused and as many defence counsel. One of the defence lawyers accused Rae of conducting the Crown's case improperly and the trial judge, Mr. Justice Edson Haines, admonished him, "You can't say things like that about the Crown Attorney!"

"Oh, no, My Lord," the prosecutor said, "please let him go on. Let him play out the rope. He'll soon hang himself with it!"

The jury laughed heartily and the judge called a recess and said he'd see all counsel in his chambers.

In chambers, one of the lawyers, David Humphrey, Q.C., of Toronto, quipped: "My Lord, when the Crown Attorney threatens to hang a defence lawyer, and the jury cheers, it's time to make a deal."

And they did.

It was arraignment day and a number of prisoners were led into a packed Edmonton courtroom to enter their pleas and elect their mode of trial – judge alone, judge without a jury or judge and jury. The charges were read to them by a court clerk who prided himself on never flubbing a line.

A prisoner stood up and the silver-tongued clerk read to him, in sonorous and ominous tones, the charge that had been brought against him. The clerk then asked the accused how he pleaded to the charge. To be precise, he said, "Do you glead pilty or not pilty?"

William Shortreed, Q.C., representing the Crown, rose quickly to his feet and to the occasion.

"My Lord," he said, "if the accused gleads pilty . . . or even if he gleads not pilty . . . I'm asking for an adjournment."

He got it, too – after the laughter had died down.

District Court Judge Barry Shapiro, of Brampton, Ontario, recalls a case he appeared in as a young lawyer, assisting the noted counsel, Isadore Levinter, Q.C., of Toronto.

Levinter called as a witness a man who was an Orthodox Jew. In deference to his religion, and in accordance with the practice then prevalent, the man was permitted to wear his hat while he swore on the Bible to tell the truth, the whole truth and nothing but the truth.

When he was finished testifying, the man went back to his seat and Levinter called his next witness, an elderly man named MacKenzie.

Mr. MacKenzie walked slowly up to the witness box. He was just about to step into the box when he stopped, turned around, retraced his steps and picked up his hat. He strolled back to the box, donned his hat and stood ready to be sworn in.

"Are you of the Jewish faith, Mr. MacKenzie?" asked the judge.

"No, My Lord, I'm not."

"Well, then, it won't be necessary for you to be sworn with your hat on."

Mr. MacKenzie took his hat off, walked slowly back to his seat, put the hat on the bench and started the trek back to the witness box.

Levinter, highly amused, as was the judge, turned to the jury and said, "I guess he's one of the members of the Lost Tribe."

Winnipeg lawyer Sydney Halter, Q.C., former Commissioner of the Canadian Football League, has an impassive face. It used to be said that though he closely resembled that old sourpuss, Charles de Gaulle, it was easy to tell them apart because de Gaulle smiled more frequently than Syd. But, as his many friends will attest, behind that scowl lurks a very friendly man.

Halter once had a gregarious paperboy who, for months on end, offered a cheery hello every time he saw him. The poor kid never received a response and he eventually decided to dispense with the greetings. The next time he saw Halter he passed by in silence.

Syd called him back.

"What's the matter?" he complained. "You mad at me?"

Now we come back, full circle, to John "Jake" Dunlap.

Jake was assisting his good friend Arthur Maloney in the defence of a man charged with robbery. In the middle of the Crown Attorney's address to the jury, the accused vomited all over himself and the prisoner's dock.

The judge adjourned court so that the mess could be cleaned up. This infuriated the Crown Attorney, who'd been stopped in his tracks by the interruption. When court resumed, he'd have to regain his concentration and his form, and he knew that the jury mightn't listen as attentively as before.

The prosecutor was sputtering with anger as he left the courtroom, followed closely by Maloney and Dunlap.

As the trio stepped into the hallway, Dunlap said in a "Shakespearean aside" to Maloney, "Did those pills ever work, eh, Arthur?"

6

They Should of Stood in Bed

"I should of stood in bed."

The philosopher who spoke those words, fight manager Joe Jacobs, said it *poifectly*. Some days, nothing goes right. And court is certainly no exception.

Take Albert Miller, for example.

One day a couple of decades ago, Miller, an eager young Toronto lawyer, was faced with a problem that arises all too frequently in the law: how to be in two places at the same time. He had to be in the Ontario Court of Appeal by 10:45 a.m. to help his boss, T.N. Phelan, Q.C., prepare for a complicated appeal he'd be arguing when the court convened fifteen minutes later. He also had to be in Small Claims Court to represent a boyhood friend who was sued by a tailor for the price of a suit, one pant-leg of which, it was alleged, was four inches shorter than the other.

"How can I swing this?" the young lawyer asked himself. "No problem," he replied. Ah, the confidence of youth!

Mr. Miller had assured his friend he'd have little trouble trouncing the tailor. Small Claims Court started at 10 a.m. and he'd be appearing before a judge who was faster than a speeding bullet. He was sure he could score a quick knock-out and make it to the Court of Appeal with plenty of time to spare. But, alas, the speedy judge he'd expected wasn't there. Pinch-hitting for him was a judge who was as slow as a turtle with a ruptured hernia.

It was 10:30 before His Honour had polished off the adjournments and at 10:45 the panic-stricken lawyer told his friend: "You'll have to defend yourself. I'll see you later."

Albert jumped in his car and raced towards Osgoode Hall, seat of the

Supreme Court of Ontario. He parked under the new City Hall, next door to Osgoode, and emerged at exactly 11 a.m.

All the law books which Mr. Phelan would require were on the "trolley" which Albert had carefully stocked the night before in the Great Library. Albert sprinted up the stairs and into the library. He grabbed the trolley with its weighty cargo of books and sped towards the courtroom.

As he entered, three learned Justices of Appeal filed in and stationed themselves on high-backed seats. Seven or eight gowned lawyers, among them some of the top counsel in Canada, waited anxiously for argument to begin.

Albert moved with unseemly haste and just as he reached the front of the courtroom he lost control of his vehicle. Every book he had lovingly stacked spewed across the floor in front of the startled judges. The young lawyer looked around in desperation. No one would give him a hand. Purple with embarrassment, he picked up all of the books and, creeping along the front of the court, he stacked them on a table near Mr. Phelan, then sat down behind his boss.

The long agonizing silence ended when the presiding judge asked testily: "Well, Mr. Phelan, are you and Mr. Miller now *quite* ready to proceed?"

Mr. Phelan rose and replied: "Yes, My Lord, we are ready." Then he leaned back towards Albert and said in a "whisper" that could be heard a block away: "Young man, you should be shot!"

Mr. Miller was so mortified he probably would have welcomed a slug between the eyes. But he got over it in jig time and today, a successful lawyer in Barrie, Ontario, he laughs heartily whenever he recalls how he desecrated the decorum of the oh-so-dignified Court of Appeal.

That's the way it is with lawyers.

"The ability of the lawyer to laugh at himself and his profession is a measure of the greatness of the profession," a writer has noted. "Whatever the reason is for this, there is probably no other profession which makes more fun of itself."

James Thurber must have been thinking of the kind of incident related above when he wrote: "Humour is emotional chaos remembered in tranquility."

Another case in point would be the riotous ride of Brantford lawyer Clifford Charles Slemin, which also culminated in a performance in the Ontario Court of Appeal. Kenneth P. Lefebvre, Q.C., of Brantford, tells the tale as follows:

"Cliff was the type of lawyer who attracted disasters, and on the day in question he arrived at his office about 9:20 to be met by a shriek from his secretary who advised him that he was scheduled to be in Osgoode Hall at 10:00 for a criminal appeal. A quick call to Osgoode to advise that Mr. Slemin would be late was followed by a panicky rounding up of the client and the client's father (both of whom wanted to be present) and Cliff set off on a sixty-five-mile journey in a convertible car.

"Counsel's memory was being refreshed by his client regarding the exact particulars of this case, as they took a shortcut, when suddenly the client's voice from the back seat was strangely muffled.

"A glance to the rear confirmed that the client had gone up through the canvas roof of the convertible when the car, travelling at one hundred miles an hour, had flown over the C.P.R. track at the last level crossing. Useful time was wasted in disengaging the client from his predicament and Cliff arrived at the robing room in a state of confusion and petulance.

"It was then discovered that he had forgotten to pack his collar, tabs or cuff links and that the judges of the Court of Appeal were showing every sign of impatience.

"Cliff decided to 'bluff it out' and so he improvised some cuff links from paper clips, pulled his robe up as far as possible over his shoulders and went into court pretending to be hunchbacked.

"Cliff loved to tell this story at bar association dinners and always concluded by saying: 'Well, I won the appeal, boys, but I was so bent over I never did find out who was sitting up there.' "

If the judges *had* noticed the woeful state of Cliff Slemin's wardrobe, they likely would have refused to hear his argument. After all, our courts are places of solemn dignity and lawyers are expected to act and dress accordingly, especially in the higher courts where they wear black gowns, wing collars and bib-like tabs.

Some judges go into a tizzy if they spot even a minor infraction of the dress code – tabs slightly askew, perhaps, or the top of a cigarette package peeking out of a vest pocket. Others are provoked only by more serious violations, such as the wearing of light-coloured pants under a gown. Many a barrister has been tossed out of the game for this sort of effrontery.

"I can't hear you," is the way judges usually put it when giving lawyers the gate. This charming phrase sometimes triggers a saucy response. On rare occasions, it has sparked replies of utter audacity.

Winnipeg lawyer Graeme Haig, Q.C., chuckles when he recalls the time his colleague, Bert Honeyman, appeared before a judge minus his tabs.

"I can't hear you, Mr. Honeyman," the judge declared.

"That old bastard's getting deafer all the time," the lawyer quipped, not at all softly, to the man beside him.

And in Windsor, Ontario, about forty years ago, a leading counsel, Gordon Fraser, Q.C., appeared before a judge who had been disliked by his colleagues when he was a lawyer and had learned since going on the Bench that things hadn't changed. Mr. Fraser, it seems, was wearing light-coloured pants under his gown.

"I can't hear you, Mr. Fraser," His Lordship announced.

Mr. Fraser spoke louder.

"I can't hear you!"

Mr. Fraser spoke even louder.

"No, no, sir, what I mean – and you know it – is that I *won't* hear you! You are improperly attired. It's an insult to the dignity of this court!"

"Very well," Mr. Fraser replied. He gathered up his papers, shoved them in his briefcase and headed for the door. He said something as he was leaving.

"What was that you just said?" the judge demanded.

"Oh, it wasn't anything important."

"Come back here! Tell me what you said!"

"You insist, My Lord?"

"Yes, in the name of this court, I insist."

"If you insist," Mr. Fraser said, walking back towards the counsel table, "then I *have* to tell you."

"That's correct."

"And you can't do anything about it."

"No, I suppose not."

"Well, I was just commenting – to myself, mind you – that the higher the monkey climbs the pole, the more you see of his big asshole!"

Sometimes a male lawyer will appear in court looking like a million bucks from the neck down but his face needs immediate attention. Unless you're a female lawyer or a man with an established beard, shaving prior to trial is an absolute must. Failure to do so can lead to the old heave-ho.

A Winnipeg lawyer once stick-handled through an entire trial with such dexterity that the judge saw only the left side of his face. He'd forgotten to shave the right side.

Another lawyer, who'd neglected to shave altogether, incurred the wrath of a magistrate, who snapped, "Counsel, why didn't you shave this morning?"

The fast-thinking lawyer retorted, "I wasn't planning on being up very long today, Your Worship."

Dignity sometimes makes a sudden exit. A few years ago, Walton Cook, Q.C., was arguing a criminal case before Provincial Court Judge Sandra Oxner in Lunenberg, Nova Scotia, when the town's fire alarm started to wail. Without any further ado, Cook, a member of the voluntary fire department, dropped everything and sprinted through the door. He re-appeared about an hour later, with his rubber boots rolled down just below his knees, and continued as if nothing had happened.

Most judges regard it as their duty to make sure that sober standards of dress and deocrum are observed in the courtroom, but some take this duty more seriously than others. Manitoba Chief Justice E.K. Williams, a fusspot on matters sartorial, often subjected counsel to severe tongue lashings when he spied something he didn't like about their appearance. Even his judicial brethren couldn't escape his censure.

Chief Justice Williams had a hang-up about brown shoes. He felt strongly that no judge should ever show up at a court house, even to do office work, wearing such undignified-looking things. His colleagues didn't all agree. Mr. Justice Ralph Maybank often wore brown shoes, and it's said that whenever he did he'd stop at the C.J.'s office and point with a malicious grin to his offending footwear.

Yet, some judges carry casualness to extremes. A few years ago a man appeared at the Provincial Court office in Winnipeg, wanting to speak to a judge whose name he couldn't recall. Efforts to describe the judge failed at first, but the staff knew who he was as soon as the man said, "He's the one who always picks his nose in court."

In Edmonton, an absent-minded Provincial Court judge came into his chambers one rainy afternoon, completed some correspondence, robed and went into court. It wasn't until court was over that he realized he had spent the afternoon in his rain coat.

The same judge came in from lunch one day, went into court and heard several cases. He wondered why no one would look at him squarely. When court was over he went back into his chambers and noticed he still had his hat on.

That's fairly mild compared with the hilarious swearing-in of a Provincial Court judge in Fredericton, New Brunswick, a few years back. The new judge was about five-foot-seven and weighed about 140 pounds. His tailor-made gown wasn't ready for the swearing-in ceremony, so he was given a gown belonging to the previous judge, a man who stood six-foot-four and weighed 260 pounds.

On his way into the courtroom, which was packed with friends, relatives, judges and lawyers, the new recruit caught the gown on a post and tore it. He retreated for necessary repairs.

On re-entry, he discovered another problem. His chair was a pivoting model which screwed in and out to adjust the height. It had been screwed right down to the bottom, to accommodate his predecessor. When he sat on it, all the audience could see of him was the top of his head. This necessitated another adjournment while the chair was readjusted.

On his third run at getting sworn in, the candidate discovered that the chair was too high and his feet didn't touch the floor. When he leaned forward to speak to the audience, his chair turned slowly to the right.

After he'd been sworn in, his secretary told him that, all things considered, the ceremony had gone quite well. Then she added, "But don't you think you should have done up your fly?"

"I don't get no respect!" is comedian Rodney Dangerfield's constant lament. He's not alone. Judges sometimes feel that way, too.

A Manitoba lawyer tells of a talk he had a few years ago in the chambers of a Supreme Court judge who is a stickler for decorum. His Lordship had just encountered a brash young practitioner and he was complaining that the younger generation of lawyers no longer treats the judiciary with the respect their office deserves.

"The youngsters just don't understand the importance of judicial dignity," he said, "the way older lawyers do."

Just then a senior lawyer stuck his head in the door and tossed the judge a greeting:

"Hi-ya, Fatso!"

Dignity, dignity. You keep hearing that word.

Courts must be dignified places; if they weren't, respect for the law would all but evaporate. But too much dignity can be a pain.

Well-known Winnipeg lawyer Harry Walsh, Q.C., had a trial before a judge who fairly dripped dignity. The trial had been in progress for several minutes when the judge suddenly left the Bench without any explanation. He returned a few minutes later and declared: "We'll have to start this trial all over again. I forgot to wear my vest!"

Dignity can disappear pretty fast. Sometimes, you might say, it's gone with the wind.

Provincial Court Judge Joseph Addison, of Toronto, recalls the time he asked a man how he pleaded to a criminal charge and the man replied with a loud fart.

Toronto lawyer Tommy Horkins jumped to his feet immediately and said: "I'm sure I speak for all counsel present when I state that we hold a much higher opinion of Your Honour than that expressed by the accused."

A Winnipeg lawyer had just finished addressing the jury and as he was resuming his place, a pungent odour spread through the courtroom.

"Dave!" his assistant whispered, not so quietly. "Did you . . .?"

"I don't think so."

They looked at the judge, who shook his head and said, "Not me."

"Sorry," said the foreman of the jury.

7

This and That

Judges, lawyers and witnesses don't get all the funny lines. Others manage to get in on the act, intentionally or otherwise.

Hon. Sam Freedman, former Chief Justice of Manitoba, recalls fondly the widow who said, "Don't talk to me about lawyers! I've had so much trouble with John's estate, why, honestly, sometimes I wish he hadn't died!"

A mother, with kids in tow, went to a Family Court office in Toronto a few years ago. One of the children had no shoes and no pants and, in no time at all, managed to perform the inevitable all over the waiting room.

"Would you please give me a diaper?" the mother asked a member of the staff.

"We don't have diapers here," was the reply.

"You have no diapers?" the mother asked with disbelief. "And you call this a Family Court!"

Back in the 1950s, court reporters in British Columbia made only a nominal salary. They fared a lot better if the Crown and defence lawyers ordered transcripts, for reporters were paid a fee for each transcript they produced. They had a vested interest in murder because in murder cases transcripts were always ordered.

In an attempted murder case, the accused became emotional as he gave evidence of firing at his son-in-law to scare him. Excitedly, he cried, "I wish now I'd killed him!"

Court reporter Don Smith, one of the most outspoken people on the west coast, looked at the witness and said, "So do I. We need the business."

A Vancouver court clerk got into the booze with counsel while a criminal jury was deliberating. He was much the worse for wear when the jury returned a verdict of guilty. "Prisoner," the clerk asked, "do you wish to say anything before His Lordship throws the book at you?"

Mr. Justice John Maher, of the Saskatchewan Court of Queen's Bench, sends this story:

"It was in the thirties and the Great Depression was at its height. John N. Conroy of North Battleford, Saskatchewan, was the solicitor for a number of farm machinery companies that held promissory notes from farmers as security for the purchase price of farm machinery.

"His instructions were to sue and attempt to recover on a large number of these notes. In those days, promissory notes had to be presented for payment and the allegation in the statement of claim was that the note was overdue, had been duly presented for payment, dishonoured and was still unpaid.

"Each statement of claim had to be typed individually and Mr. Conroy's secretary, who had a bit of a reputation as a party girl, was busy typing them on a Tuesday morning following a long holiday weekend.

"When Mr. Conroy arrived at the office, he noted the secretary appeared a little 'hung over' and after greeting her he said, 'How are you feeling this morning?' Her reply was, 'Just like these promissory notes – overdue, dishonoured and unpaid!' "

Mr. Justice George Noble, also of the Saskatchewan Court of Queen's Bench, has a yarn he entitles "The Three 'F's' – A True Story." I can't improve on it, so here it is, the way I got it:

"The plaintiff, a fortyish woman on the hefty side, had sued for damages arising out of the rear end collision which she alleged had left her with a painful and debilitating whiplash, particularly in the area of her right neck and shoulder.

"At trial, before a judge and jury, her counsel led her through the usual evidence about the cause of her injury, the pain and suffering that had resulted, and then turned his questioning to the disruption and diminishment of her lifestyle. He commenced by exploring with her the kinds of recreation she had taken part in before the accident and followed by eliciting from her a description of how each recreation had been affected by her injury.

"The plaintiff first described for the jury that she had always been very musical and had for many years played the violin, indeed had played in an orchestra for public dancing. However, since the accident she found her neck and shoulder so sore it made it impossible to any longer enjoy playing the violin.

"'What else did you do?' asked counsel.

"'Well,' she said, 'My husband and I used to fish together a lot for steelhead and trout.' She explained that their habit was to use steel lines but since her injury she was no longer capable of handling the lines and had been forced to give it up.

"After leading her through two or three other areas of recreation, with much the same story to tell, counsel came to the question of her sex life after the injury.

"'Oh!' she said, 'it's simply terrible.' In fact she claimed her sexual activity had been so diminished by her injury that she seriously wondered if her marriage would hold together very much longer.

"The clerk of the court, sitting directly in front of the judge, apparently had been listening to this tale of woe by the plaintiff with some interest. He scribbled a note and handed it to the judge who opened it during a lull in the plaintiff's testimony to read:

"'Life just ain't worth living if you can't fish, fiddle or fuck!'

"The outcome of the trial may have reflected the clerk's bemused comment, for the jury, in the end, gave the plaintiff less damages than the amount of money the defendants had paid into court to settle the claim."

Robert D. McIntyre, Q.C., of Brampton, Ontario, has a dandy:

"Some years ago when I had a smaller office I hired a bookkeeper who occasionally would act as receptionist. As with all bookkeepers, I had impressed upon her the necessity of keeping an accurate firm trust account.

"One day, while sitting at the receptionist's desk, the very concerned bookkeeper was trying to reconcile the year-end trust account and no matter what she did it came out thirty-eight cents short.

"She went for a coffee break, where she expressed her concern to one of my secretaries, and then returned to the receptionist's desk. At that moment, coincidentally, an Ontario Provincial Police client came into the office in uniform. At this point, my bookkeeper screamed to the perplexed officer: 'My God, it's only thirty-eight cents!' "

George R. Baker, Editor of the Senate Debates, used to be a court reporter. He recalls a time he dined with a cranky Supreme Court of Ontario judge who treated his so-called inferiors with disdain.

The judge was rude and unkind to the waiter and Baker went to see the man later and apologized for the boorish behaviour of his boss.

"Don't worry, sir," the waiter said. "With people like that we can always spit in their soup – and we do!"

Serge Kujawa, Q.C., Associate Deputy Minister of Justice in the Saskatchewan government, and prosecutor in the sensational Colin Thatcher murder case, loves to tell this story on himself. One day a few years ago, Serge was a few seconds late for court. As he entered the court-room he heard the defence lawyer saying: "I appear for the accused, My Lord. I'm ready to proceed."

"Who's appearing for the prosecution?" asked the judge.

"Mr. Kujawa," answered a policeman who sat beside the prosecu-tor's empty chair.

"You don't look like Mr. Kujawa," His Lordship quipped.

"Thank you," the officer said.

Ronald Shatford was a real "baddie," but he was a friendly fellow and he had a great sense of humour. In the early 1970s, he sat in a Toronto courtroom one day and waited for the imminent arrival of the dreaded Judge Walter Martin, who was going to sentence him for armed robbery.

While he waited to learn his fate, Shatford chatted with court clerk Jack Hughes.

"Jack," he said, "I feel like a new bride."

"Why's that, Ron?" Hughes asked.

"I know it's coming, but I don't know how long it's gonna be."

(Seconds before Judge Martin hoved into view, Shatford flashed all his fingers and thumbs twice, thus indicating that he thought he'd get twenty years. He was right on.)

Provincial Court Judge Blake Lynch, of Fredericton, New Brunswick, tells about a man who asked if his minor traffic case could be heard early so he could get back to work.

It was about 9:15 a.m. when the man made the request. Judge Lynch said he couldn't hear the matter until court opened at ten but he would accommodate him by taking him first. He asked him to take a seat in court.

As the man walked away, agitated, he said under his breath, "Asshole!"

Judge Lynch heard this and he cited the man for contempt of court and had him put in the cells.

Later the prisoner said he wanted to apologize and he was taken back before the judge.

"I'm sorry, Your Honour," he said. "I was having a terrible day."

Judge Lynch asked him how he would have reacted if *he'd* been the judge and heard an accused call him "an arsehole."

"I didn't call you an arsehole," the man protested. "I called you an asshole."

(There's a difference? Either way, it was a pretty cheeky thing to say.)

Tupper Bigelow, who was a magistrate and Provincial Court Judge in Toronto for thirty-two years, recalls a Basque who appeared before him charged with a minor offence. When arraigned on the charge, the man said, "Me Basque. No spik Anglese."

"He could speak English okay at the station last night," said the arresting officer.

Nevertheless, Bigelow ordered that the accused should have a Basque interpreter at his trial, and he remanded him for a week on his own bail. A week later, there was still no Basque interpreter in court. Indeed, said the Crown Attorney, there was no such thing in Toronto.

"This case will be dismissed," Judge Bigelow declared.

Immediately the man headed for the door. When he got there, he turned and looked at the judge, smiled sweetly and said, "Thanks a lot, Your Honour."

Mr. Bigelow also tells of a young woman who testified at the preliminary hearing of a rape case in Toronto. She said a man picked her up when she was hitchhiking, took her to a remote area and raped her.

"How did you get home?" the Crown Attorney asked her. "Did you take a taxi?"

"No," she said, "I *told* you before that's why I hitchhiked – I didn't have any money."

"But how did you get home? By public transport?"

"No, I told you I didn't have any money or a streetcar ticket," the woman said with exasperation, "so I hitchhiked."

"You hitchhiked *again*! Weren't you afraid of being raped again?"

"Oh, no," she said nonchalantly. "I didn't think lightning would strike twice. And, besides, he was an old guy of about thirty!"

Thirty, indeed! If she wants to see "old guys," she should drop in on some of our divorce courts.

Judge Peter Nicholson, of the County Court of Annapolis County, Nova Scotia, heard a case a few years ago in which a seventy-nine-year-old man petitioned for a divorce from his fifty-two-year-old wife. He had "met" her two years earlier via ham radio – he was in Nova Scotia, she was in Texas – and this led to letter-writing and then holy deadlock. He soon discovered that his bride was a prostitute, with clients all over Texas. She gave him VD, took almost everything he had and then told him to get lost. The last Judge Nicholson heard of the man was two years later when, pushing eighty-one, he was engaged to a young woman with three small children. She lived in the Philippines. They'd met through a pen pal club.

Trevor Alexander, a lawyer in Victoria, British Columbia, represented an eighty-seven-year-old man who petitioned for divorce on the ground of mental cruelty. He told the court that his wife placed an ironing board between them in the matrimonial bed and, worse, washed his socks several times in dishwater stained with gravy. When the judge heard that, he turned crimson, covered his head with his hands and said, "Oh, my, that's the cruellest thing I've heard in years!"

The man got his divorce decree. It's not known whether he committed matrimony again.

And speaking of divorce, in a case heard in Walkerton, Ontario, about thirty years ago, two private detectives gave the standard sort of private-eye evidence pertaining to adultery. The ever-cranky Mr. Justice Fred Barlow threw the case out, saying he was familiar with the detectives and didn't believe a word they said. He then called a short recess.

During the recess, a lawyer saw a young woman sobbing uncontrollably. He was deeply touched and went over and spoke to her.

"Were you the plaintiff in the last case?" he asked.

"No," she replied, "I'm the plaintiff in the next case, and I have the same witnesses!"

Martin H. Bushell was another person who had witness problems. Martin is the Public Trustee of the Province of Nova Scotia, but back in 1954, when this story unfolded, he was a rookie lawyer in Halifax who was mighty anxious about his first divorce case. He tells us about it:

"My client, the plaintiff in an uncontested action for divorce, was with me on our way to the Court House. I stopped en route at a local hotel for my first interview with a witness who had previously been questioned by an investigator on my behalf and had made a signed statement admitting adultery with the respondent.

"He was undoubtedly the respondent's lover but though both he and a corroborative witness were subpoenaed from a distant town to testify on behalf of the plaintiff, the corroborative witness could not be located. So proof of adultery would depend solely upon the lover's evidence.

"I confronted him in his hotel room scarcely an hour before the trial was scheduled to begin. I handed him a copy of my investigator's report and asked him if it was a fair summary of the evidence he would give at trial.

"He contemptuously tore the paper to shreds and, gesturing towards two male companions, threatened me as follows: 'My friends and I need twenty-five dollars for gas and expenses to get us back to New Glasgow. If you want me to talk for your judge, you gotta pay me now!'

"Since his travelling expenses, including one night's hotel accommodation, had been handed to him with the subpoena, I thought a tough stand was called for.

"With as much severity as I could muster, I replied, 'Mister, you're bound by subpoena to testify at the trial. The sheriff will take you there by force if necessary. I have another copy of that paper with your signature on it. You had better be on the witness stand as soon as your name is called and you had better tell the truth or I'll show my copy to the judge and you'll see the inside of a jail cell before you next see New Glasgow.'

"Then, glowing with self-righteousness, I led my client away to the Court House and left him, with a few short words of encouragement, in a waiting room while I went to the barristers' room to gown.

"Moments later we were all in court. I admit to feeling uneasy as our witness took the stand, but his testimony conformed exactly to the investigator's report and evidently satisfied the judge, whose only comment was, 'Decree nisi granted.'

"Congratulating my client as we left the courtroom, I added, 'So, our witness decided to behave himself. There's only one way to handle a fellow like that!'

"My sense of enormous self-satisfaction was deflated when he replied, 'Yeah, while you were inside puttin' on that vulture suit, I paid him the twenty-five bucks!'"

A Barrie, Ontario, lawyer, Edward Wildman, tells about a fellow who wasn't too swift. Appearing in court in Collingwood, Ontario, the man pleaded guilty to ten break-and-enter charges. The judge sentenced him to two months, consecutive, on each charge.

"How much time did I get?" he asked the arresting officer on the way to jail.

"You got twenty months," the officer replied.

The prisoner thought about it for a minute, then smiled and said, "Oh, well, it coulda been worse. I coulda got a year!"

Nervousness gives rise to many unintentionally humorous remarks in court:

A Vancouver courtroom was packed with lawyers, waiting to present motions to a Supreme Court judge. The clerk called the first case of the day and a young barrister stepped forward jauntily, trying to fight off the nervousness that consumed him, and determined to make a good impression.

Since he was the "lead-off batter," the young man thought he should start with a salutation of some sort. He bowed slightly to the judge, opened his mouth to speak and surprised everyone, especially himself, with these words:

"Good morning, my love."

The judge smiled and replied, "No one calls me 'my love' until he's at least a Q.C."

In Toronto many years ago, a cantankerous judge gave a prominent young lawyer a very rough ride on all his arguments. He interrupted counsel repeatedly, gave his own rendition of what the law was, and asked demandingly, "Isn't that so?"

The lawyer, thoroughly shaken and probably thinking of other arguments before another forum, answered, "Yes, dear."

The late Mr. Justice Fred Barlow, who intimidated many an Ontario lawyer with his churlish interruptions, reduced one counsel to silence. His Lordship cut into the man's argument and barked: "Come, come, Mr. Gogo!" Mr. Gogo was so flustered he didn't know whether he was coming or going. He decided to go – back to his seat.

The late Arthur Maloney, Q.C., was castigated, early in his career, by Mr. Justice Barlow. Maloney was so rattled by the rebuke that he forgot where he was. He sat down angrily at the counsel table, lit a cigarette and started smoking. This led to another Barlow blast, twice as bad as the one before.

Mr. Justice Barlow once lectured a young witness as follows:

"Now, when you answer my question you don't just say 'Yes' or 'No.' There's a proper form of address in the courts in Ontario. In Magistrates' Court it's 'Yes, Your Worship.' In County Court it's 'Yes, Your Honour.' In the High Court it's 'Yes, My Lord' or 'Yes, Your Lordship.' Now, what is your answer?"

"Yes, my God," the flustered witness replied.

I once gave a similar rundown to a client who was nervous about testifying, adding that if he couldn't remember which form of address to use he'd be all right if he just said "Sir." Kiddingly, I said, "But whatever you do, don't call the judge Your Majesty."

Oh, the power of suggestion! The first time the judge asked him a question, my client said, "Yes, Your Majesty."

For quite some time, a young lawyer managed to avoid appearing before his mother, who is a member of the Court of Queen's Bench of one of our western provinces. One day, though, he had to appear before her on a routine chambers matter. His case headed the list and the lawyers in attendance were anxious to hear what he'd say. He was so nervous he said:

"Good morning, Your Honour . . . I mean . . . My Lord . . . I mean . . . Your Ladyship . . ."

"You mean 'Mother,' " said the judge.

Oh, well, you might say, what's in a name? Ask the fellow who prosecuted the next case. Better still, ask the accused.

On April 11, 1983, in Toronto, a man appeared before Provincial Court Judge Milton Cadsby on charges of careless driving and failing to remain at the scene of an accident. My thanks to Toronto lawyer Gunter Vordemberge for sending me a transcript of the festivities. It shows the following conversation between the Crown Attorney and the judge:

CROWN: Your Honour, the fail to remain charge actually involves a vehicle driven by the accused striking a rabbit. Having of the view that the rabbit is not in the category of cattle . . .
COURT: He what? He hit a what?
CROWN: The vehicle struck a rabbit, so (since I am) of the view that a rabbit is not of the category of cattle, I ask that charge be withdrawn, Your Honour.
COURT: Let me see that information.
CROWN: I should indicate, Your Honour, the rabbit is in fact owned. It is not a wild type of rabbit, it is owned by someone.
COURT: The charge is the same as a dog, if you strike a dog. Anyway, he's charged with leaving the scene of an accident after an accident with a vehicle. You're withdrawing that charge?
CROWN: I'm withdrawing that charge.
COURT: That's the one you're withdrawing?
CROWN: Well, probably there is some mistake in the wording of the information.

COURT: Well, the information refers to a vehicle.

CROWN: Yes, my understanding is that incident actually involved a rabbit, rather than a vehicle.

COURT: I see. That's a good reason to withdraw it. That charge is marked withdrawn.

The Crown Attorney then spoke to the investigating officer and learned that the accused's vehicle had, in fact, struck a Volkswagen Rabbit.

Kevin Carroll, Q.C., of Barrie, Ontario, tells of another case in which a name meant a lot:

A Toronto man, suspected of being the "connection" for several big international drug dealers, was under surveillance by the R.C.M.P. and the Drug Squad of the Metropolitan Toronto police. One night, a team of "narcs," as drug police are known, staked out the man's house near High Park, in the west end of Toronto. They'd heard that a big drug deal was about to happen and they figured the suspect would lead them to the action.

As police lurked in the shadows, the man left his house, walking his dog towards High Park. The officers slinked ahead and hid behind bushes and trees in the inky blackness of the park.

Man and beast strolled through the park, oblivious to the forms which slithered and crouched nearby.

Suddenly the man cried out, "Narc! Narc! Narc!"

Police swarmed out of hiding, seized the man and slapped on the cuffs.

"I don't know why you're bothering me," the prisoner declared. "I was just calling my dog."

Really and truly, the mutt was named "Narc."

"Martinize" is–or at least it was–another name with two meanings. It's the name given to a method of dry-cleaning, but in Toronto in the 1960s and '70s, it was also the name of a brand of justice that struck terror in the hearts of men who swiped money at gun-point.

Walter Martin, a tall, beefy man who was once a Canadian tennis champion, was Senior County Court Judge for the County of York. When it came to sentencing criminals, especially bank robbers, Martin was a "heavy hitter" – the heaviest around.

A notorious Montreal bandit, Claude Pion, appeared before Judge Martin in the early 1970s, charged with knocking off a Toronto bank. Pion, who represented himself, asked that his trial be conducted in

French. In those days there was no absolute right to a French trial in Toronto, as there is now. Judge Martin noted that Pion spoke adequate English and he assured him that he'd explain anything that might need explaining.

Pion insisted that the confession presented by the Crown had been forced out of him by Toronto police, who, he said, had burned his testicles with a lighted cigar. After hearing all the evidence on the subject, Judge Martin ruled that the confession had been given voluntarily, and the trial proceeded.

The accused also complained that he was being "Martinized."

"What does that mean?" asked Judge Martin, who said he'd never heard the term.

"Oh, come on, Your Honour, you must know what I mean," Pion replied.

"No, I don't. Tell me."

So Pion told him: For some time, Toronto police had been warning holdup artists that if they didn't plead guilty before another judge, they'd be tried by Judge Walter Martin, who would send them away for a long, long stretch. This was known as "Martinizing," Pion explained.

After a trial that took a month, Pion was found guilty. The Crown presented his record – four convictions for armed robbery, four very long vacations.

"You wanted to hear some French," Judge Martin said. "Here's your sentence in French – *c'est la vie!*"

Roger Caron, a hardened criminal who later reformed and wrote a best-selling book about the Canadian penal system, was sentenced to twenty-five years by Judge Martin, who thoughtfully added this greeting:

"Welcome to the Quarter-Century Club!"

One night about ten years ago, Judge Martin participated in a mock trial that was filmed for educational television at Osgoode Hall Law School, on the outskirts of Toronto. Filming started about seven o'clock at night and ended about eight hours later. Judge Martin played the judge in the film, a top-flight production that's still shown occasionally. Bob McGee, Q.C., Deputy Crown Attorney for Metropolitan Toronto, played the prosecutor. Other parts were performed by real-life lawyers, police officers and court officials. The accused and some of the witnesses were portrayed by actors.

About three a.m., Judge Martin, still wearing his gown and tabs, got into his big white Cadillac and started driving towards the centre of the city. He had two passengers – prosecutor Bob McGee, who was also still wearing his gown and tabs, and Billy Eck, an eighty-five-year-old sheriff's officer resplendent in tails, wing collar and white tie. Billy, who sat in the back, had also been in the movie. Following behind in another car were Jack Hughes, a court clerk who played a court clerk in the film, and a police sergeant who had also been before the cameras.

Judge Martin had eye trouble and so he always drove very slowly. As the Caddy crawled down Keele Street, it caught the attention of a rookie police constable who concluded that the driver thereof must be impaired. He pulled the car over to the curb.

The constable peered into the car at the three strangely dressed men, sniffing in vain for the aroma of alcohol.

"May I see your licence?" he asked the driver.

Judge Martin handed over his wallet.

"That will tell you who I am," he said.

The officer didn't "twig" to his identity.

Judge Martin remembered that his licence plates started with the letters "C.C.J.," which stood for "County Court Judge."

"Haven't you noticed my licence plates?" His Honour hinted.

Bob McGee, who has a hearty laugh, began laughing heartily.

The officer wasn't concerned about the plates. He was checking Martin's car insurance. McGee whiled away the time chortling.

"Your insurance has expired," the constable announced. "I'll have to take you down to the station."

Judge Martin blew his stack. He started yelling at the officer. The more he yelled, the more McGee chortled.

"Where have you people been, dressed like that?" the young man asked.

"We've been at Osgoode Hall Law School filming a movie," Judge Martin advised.

"Oh, sure, I bet!" the rookie replied.

Just then, Jack Hughes and the police sergeant, who'd been following, came upon the scene.

The sergeant pulled the constable aside and the conversation, as reported later, went like this:

"Son, do you know who you've got here?"

"No, I don't. He tells me he's been filming a movie. That's got to be bullshit."

"Have you ever heard of the term 'Martinizing?' "

"Yes, I have. It has something to do with cleaning clothes."

"Well, in your case it doesn't have anything to do with cleaning clothes. If you continue with this investigation, you're going to be Martinized. Now get lost!"

He did.

In the early 1920s, an eminent Ontario lawyer, Dick Greer, was defending a man charged with the rape of a prostitute. He was assisted by his young partner, John Cartwright, who later became Chief Justice of Canada.

The trial judge, who was rather forceful in his opinions, was critical of Greer's cross-examination of a witness on the subject of whether it was customary to pay before or after the act. His Lordship gave the jury his own opinion on the matter. Cartwright whispered to Greer that he thought the judge was wrong and Greer amused the jury with what he "whispered" back: "Don't worry, John, that's just been *his* experience."

Mr. Justice John Arnup, of the Ontario Court of Appeal, recalls an appeal brought in that court in the 1930s by a woman convicted of keeping a common bawdy house. Counsel was attacking the evidence of a police informer who had gone to the premises. He testified that he'd been admitted by the accused and taken to the second floor, where he enjoyed the favours of a girl, then paid her two dollars and left.

As soon as this evidence was referred to, a member of the court, the late Mr. Justice W.T. Henderson, exclaimed, "How could anyone possibly believe a man like that? Everybody knows you pay *downstairs!*"

I'm indebted to court reporter Gail McGilvray, who preserved for posterity these immortal words of a judge of the Supreme Court of Ontario: "I don't want to pre-judge the thing; I just want to indicate I've got my mind made up, that's all."

David C. Day, Q.C., of St. John's, tells of a Newfoundland magistrate who used to call court to order by rapping a fifty-cent piece on the bench. When asked why he did this, His Worship replied:

"LET ME TELL YOU WHY I RAP A FIFTY-CENT PIECE ON MY BENCH—

WELL, FIRSTLY, IT'S SHINY AND ATTRACTS ATTENTION...

... SECONDLY, I LIKE THE RESONANT SOUND IT MAKES WHEN I RAP IT ON MY BENCH...

..THIRDLY, IT CONTAINS THE QUEEN'S LIKENESS, IN KEEPING WITH MY ROLE AS ONE OF HER MAJESTY'S MAGISTRATES...

... AND, FOURTHLY...

...IT HELPS ME MAKE UP MY MIND ON THE EVIDENCE."

8

Boys
Will Be
Boys

"May I have your attention, please?"

A hundred or so judges stopped chatting and tuned in to the man at the front of the ballroom.

"Our guest speaker's plane has arrived and he'll be here in a few minutes," announced Judge Harry Williams. "While we're waiting, there are a few interesting things I wish to tell you about this unusual man."

The scene was an Ottawa hotel; the date, June 7, 1974. The judges were members of the Ontario Provincial Court (Criminal Division), assembled for their annual conference. The man who would address them at luncheon was listed on the program as Sir Hrundi V. Bashki, of the Bar of New Delhi.

Judge Williams and Judge Tom Swabey, organizers of the conference, had been singing the praises of this speaker for several days, stating that he was one of the most brilliant men in India and well worth hearing. Two of their brethren said they'd heard Bashki speak in England and were eager to hear him again.

"Our speaker was called to the bar when he was only fourteen years old," Judge Williams told the waiting jurists. "He had the highest marks ever attained in an Indian law school – averaging 99.1 percent! He became a Queen's Counsel when he was nineteen. His Q.C. had to be held in trust for him by the Great India Tea and Trust Company until he reached twenty-one. He's a fascinating man, but I want to warn you that he's quite eccentric."

Moments later, Sir Hrundi V. Bashki arrived. As he approached the ballroom, a senior judge who had just heard Judge Williams' comments stepped aside reverently. Bashki was a swarthy, slender man with jet black hair slicked down and parted in the middle. He wore short pants, knee socks, a seersucker jacket and dark glasses. He was flanked by two red-coated officers of the Royal Canadian Mounted Police.

The judges stood and applauded as the Mounties escorted the visiting dignitary to the head table.

In introducing the speaker, Judge Williams was rhapsodic. It appeared that Bashki had almost every degree imaginable – *summa cum laude*, of course – and he had lectured at every great law school in the world. He'd had an exciting, immensely successful career at the bar and there was hardly a legal topic that he wasn't a leading authority on.

So why, in God's name, did he chose to speak about German legal philosophy? The subject wasn't exactly a "grabber." Oh well, Judge Williams *had* warned that this fellow was eccentric.

On and on the speaker droned, reading from a thick sheaf of papers. With his heavy Indian accent, it was difficult to tell what he was saying. It sounded like gibberish. Whatever he was saying, the judges seemed mesmerized by the man.

Starved for recognition, Bashki started "working" the crowd. Several times he stopped in the middle of a sentence, looked at the audience, flashed a smile, waved his arms and coaxed some applause. At the rear of the room, Judge Swabey nearly choked to death from laughing.

Suddenly, Bashki went into a rage and screamed, "You're all a bunch of dummies! You don't understand a word I've been saying!"

He threw his papers at the audience and sat down in a huff.

About half the judges laughed. The others sat in silent bewilderment, still not in on the joke.

The visitor then leaped to his feet and launched into a breathless account of his career at the New Delhi bar, including a murder case he defended in which the accused, fresh out of money, had given him three of his wives in part payment of his fees. During court recess, Bashki said, he relaxed by "fondling my retainers."

After several more minutes of hilarious hooey, the speaker whipped off his dark glasses and it was announced that Sir Hrundi V. Bashki, of the New Delhi bar, was really Mr. Colin D. McKinnon, of the Ottawa bar.

The room rocked with laughter. Everyone agreed it was a masterful performance. Once in a blue moon a lawyer puts one over on a judge. But to fool a roomful of judges, and win their applause as well, is probably unprecedented. It's proof positive of the old adage that "bullshit baffles brains."

Colin McKinnon, Q.C., is a charming fellow whose playful dialects have been well received in the nation's capital – but not by everyone. After word got around about his caper with the judges, Colin was contacted by Ottawa mayor Pierre Benoit, who had lined up an interesting new gig for him.

Attired in his Bashki get-up, and using the Bashki handle, McKinnon addressed the annual private dinner of Ottawa's aldermen and Board of Control. His topic was sewage control in New Delhi – a fitting subject for India's "Minister of Sewage."

Events proceeded pretty much as before, except this time Bashki skipped the tirade.

"I got an incredibly polite hearing," McKinnon says, "but when I was introduced by Pierre as being me, one senior Board of Control member was so incensed he wanted to beat me up. Pierre, who used to play football, intervened and with the help of another politician got me out safely!"

How do you like that? A fellow tries to jolly up the world a bit and some spoilsport wants to break his face. Have we become so serious that we have no time left for merriment and tomfoolery? Are pranks passé?

Fortunately, no. We've always had them, and we always will. Inside every "adult" there's a child struggling to get out. If the kid makes it, now and then, the adult has a fairly good chance of keeping his or her marbles. That applies in the legal world, too. *Especially* in the legal world, which is so terribly, terribly serious that sometimes you could just *scream*!

Believe it or not, judges are human. They like to have fun, just like anyone else.

Take Judge Warren Durham, for instance. Judge Durham is a member of the Provincial Court (Family Division) in Brampton, Ontario. One day in 1977 he disqualified himself from hearing a husband-wife "non-support" case, saying he knew the people involved. Judge John Allen, who'd only recently been sworn in, was sent from Oshawa to Brampton to hear the case. The two judges had never met.

The pinch-hitting judge soon found that he had his hands full. The husband was a dithering, incoherent fellow in coveralls and sneakers. The wife was a shrew who sniped at her spouse throughout the proceedings. A court reporter took down every word that was said.

When he'd heard all the evidence and ruled on the case, Judge Allen dropped into Judge Durham's office to introduce himself. Judge Durham was there – wearing coveralls, sneakers and a big, wide grin. The rest of the "cast" were there too, the court reporter and Judge Durham's regular court clerk, who had starred in the role of the wife. There's no business like show business.

Judge Allen had been well and truly sucked in, but he laughed just as heartily as the others.

In northern Alberta, about twenty-five years ago, another pinch-hitter went into a game that *wasn't* rigged and hit a home run. Here's what happened:

It was opening day at the judicial "ballpark" and, as usual, divorce cases were up first. A portly lawyer who'd had quite a few drinks decided that before going to bat he should have a little snooze. But, first, he reckoned, he should reread his file.

The lawyer took a couple of law books for a pillow and laid down on a table in the barristers' room. Almost immediately, he fell into a deep sleep.

When the lawyer's case was called, he couldn't be roused. Another lawyer took the man's file and familiarized himself with it. He sought out the client, quickly interviewed him and his witness, presented the evidence in court and obtained a divorce decree.

While the client's "real" lawyer slept on, the pinch-hitter had the decree typed up and signed by the judge. He then placed the file, and the decree, on the ample stomach of the comatose counsel.

When Sleeping Beauty finally came to, he couldn't help noticing that there was a decree nisi near at hand. He ran his bloodshot eyes over the document and made a remark that Alberta lawyers still recall with glee:

"That's the easiest decree I've ever obtained!"

I have it on excellent authority that until the day he died, many years later, the lawyer still wasn't aware that anyone else had had a hand in the matter. Yes, sir, sometimes truth really is stranger than fiction.

Some trials are so dull it's hard for the judge to keep his mind on the evidence. In one such case, tried at Peace River, Alberta, a judge of the Court of Queen's Bench divided his time between listening to the dreary evidence and gazing out the window.

From his vantage point, His Lordship could see a much-talked-about landmark, "Kauffman's Hill," rising on the outskirts of town. It was said locally that no virgin ever walked up Kauffman's Hill, and, for positive certain, no virgin ever walked down it.

At the noon recess, the judge entertained court officials with his description of what he'd seen as he sat through the tiresome testimony. He said he'd watched a couple go up Kauffman's Hill, watched them through their endearing sojourn at the top, and then watched them come down again. His Lordship said he couldn't swear as to what had happened, because the hill was too far away, but he believed he had confirmation of the truth of the local legend.

When the judge returned to court for the afternoon session he also had confirmation of the thoughtfulness and consideration of his court reporter, Russ Klesko. There, on the Bench, was just what he needed – a pair of powerful binoculars.

Calgary lawyer Paddy Nolan, the old smoothie, loved a good prank. Here's a rather elaborate one he was involved in at the turn of the century, as described by Winnipeg lawyer and writer Roy St. George Stubbs:

"Paddy Nolan bore a striking resemblance to the Honourable T. Mayne Daly, one-time Minister of the Interior, later a police magistrate in Winnipeg. The resemblance between Nolan and Daly led to them being frequently mistaken for each other.

"When Daly was Minister of the Interior he was once approached by an irate farmer who asked him why he was not attending to his lawsuit. Realizing that the farmer had mistaken him for Nolan, Daly thought that he saw an opening for some fun, so he replied, 'Well, that certainly was a pretty rank case of yours and we weren't very favourably impressed either with you or the amount of money you sent. We are not in the law business for the good of our health, so you had better come through with some more money if you want such a case as that attended to.'

"A few days later Nolan received a letter from the farmer, pleading with him to carry on with the case. A cheque for a substantial amount accompanied the letter. At first Nolan could not make head nor tail of the matter but he finally put two and two together and waited his turn to even the score with Daly.

"He did not have to wait long. Shortly afterwards he was tackled by an angry homesteader in Lethbridge, who asked him when in the name of all things holy he was going to get his patent for his homestead.

" 'Do you think,' replied Nolan, 'that we are running the Department of the Interior for the good of our health? If you want your patent you will have to dip down in your pocket and grease our paw. Get busy and send us something worthwhile and then we can consider your patent, but till then there will be nothing moving.'

"Properly humbled, the homesteader went his way. A day or two later, Nolan received a telegram from Daly saying, 'You had better cut it out. The Department is getting a bad name.' "

Hanging on the wall of a rural Alberta courthouse was a copy of the warrant to execute King Charles II. The late R.A. Gordon, Q.C., who had a keen sense of humour, copied the warrant. In the place of King Charles he inserted the name of the local District Court judge. Then he went to see said judge.

"Good day, Your Honour," the lawyer said. "I have an order for your execution."

Those words wouldn't have rattled the judge. "Execution" is another word – a common one in legal circles – for "signature" or "signing."

The judge, an easygoing man, barely glanced at the documents.

"Are your papers all in order?" he asked.

"Yes, Your Honour," the lawyer replied.

The judge, knowing that Gordon's papers were usually shipshape, reached for his pen and signed his own death warrant.

Gordon treasured that document until the day he died. No wonder.

One day about fifteen years ago, Provincial Court Judge Joseph L. Addison was cleaning up a lot of deskwork in his office in Toronto's Old City Hall. A court clerk brought him a big batch of warrants he'd prepared and Judge Addison, as always, signed each one quickly without pausing to examine any of them.

A few hours later, Judge Addison was visited by Police Sergeant Dougall McKay, who was in charge of the lockup at Old City Hall, where many of Toronto's Provincial Court courtrooms are located. Sergeant McKay had a big, burly policeman with him.

"Good afternoon, Your Honour," McKay said when the men entered.

"Hello, Dougall," Judge Addison said affably. "what can I do for you?"

"We've come to take you to the cells, Your Honour," the Sergeant said.

"What?" the judge asked with disbelief.

"I have a warrant for your arrest, on a charge of committing an act of gross indecency."

"Let me see that thing!" said the judge. "There must be some mis–"

Sgt. McKay started to laugh – and gave the game away.

Judge Addison looked at the warrant. Sure enough, it named him. And sure enough, he was charged with "committing an act of gross indecency."

It was signed, too – by Judge Joseph L. Addison.

A famous English case, decided in 1863, became the backdrop for an imaginative prank pulled by a Calgary lawyer more than 110 years later. A certain Mr. Byrne was walking past the shop of a certain Mr. Boadle, a dealer in flour, when a barrel of flour fell from a window above the shop and seriously injured him. "*Res ipsa loquitur,*" said the court. In English, that means "the thing speaks for itself."

Byrne v. *Boadle* decided for all time that in certain situations a plaintiff doesn't have to prove that a negligent act has been committed. "A barrel could not roll out of a warehouse without some negligence," the judge declared, "and to say that a plaintiff who is injured by it must call witnesses from the warehouse to prove negligence seems to me preposterous."

Calgary lawyer Dwayne Rowe saw in *Byrne* v. *Boadle* a wonderful opportunity to have some fun. He wrote a letter to a staid, long-established Calgary law firm, stating that he acted for a Mr. Byrne (giving his full name) who was injured by a falling keg of flour outside the premises of their flour-merchant client, Mr. Boadle. He gave the real-life Mr. Boadle's full name and threw in a fictional Calgary address as the site of the mishap.

In all other respects, he recited the facts exactly as they appear in the famous judgement that's been studied by every first-year law student for the past century.

For several days, some of the juniors in the big firm were in a flap, attempting to find the file, phoning Rowe for further information, trying to locate their "client." They didn't twig to the fact that the "case" was a carbon copy of *Byrne* v. *Boadle* and that Rowe was putting them on. When a senior partner was consulted he recognized it immediately as a hoax and told the perpetrator to "stop wasting our time." He did, because, what the hell, the jig was up.

Donald A. Kerr, Q.C., of Halifax, played an imaginative and intricate practical joke on a colleague in the middle of a serious criminal case. Let's call the colleague Jones.

Jones was defending a man charged with misappropriation of funds. It was in the early days of photocopying, and the accused had produced what purported to be a photocopy of a receipt, bearing an illegible signature. The Crown contended that the receipt was a fake.

Kerr dropped into court one day while Jones was attempting to establish, through an expert, that the photocopy was genuine and that, indeed, fakery would be easily detectable. Kerr returned to his office and pulled from a file a recent one-sentence letter he'd received from Jones. It was on Jones' letterhead and was signed by Jones.

"After an hour on the photocopy machine, I was able to produce an absolutely perfect forgery," Kerr says in a letter to me. (He tells how he did it, but I'm not going to pass on *that* sort of information.)

As a result of his tinkering, Kerr now had a letter addressed to him, on Jones' letterhead and signed by Jones, the text of which read:

"TO WHOM IT MAY CONCERN: This is to certify that I am a horse's ass, and also that photocopied documents can be faked easily."

Kerr returned to court and, at a critical moment in Jones' address to the jury, prevailed upon a court attendant to pass him the sealed envelope.

Jones paused, tore open the envelope, read the letter and thundered, "What in hell is this?"

"What is it?" asked the trial judge, Mr. Justice L.D. Currie.

"It's nothing, My Lord," said Jones, trying to stuff the letter into his pocket.

"Let me see it," demanded His Lordship.

With great reluctance, Jones passed up the note.

His Lordship spotted Kerr in the audience and, knowing his proclivity for pranks, figured that he was the instigator.

"I think the jury should see this," the judge said, looking straight at Kerr.

"No, no, My Lord," Jones protested. "It's obviously a fa . . . a spuri . . . Well, it really has nothing to do with the case."

I'll let Kerr finish the tale:

" 'Perhaps you're right,' said His Lordship without a smile, putting the letter in his pocket. But I noticed that throughout the balance of the afternoon, the distinguished jurist's hand occasionally came up to cover his mouth, and his shoulders shook a little from time to time."

PART TWO

Yesteryear

9

Frontier Justice

Pierre had the hots for Marie, and vice versa.

They slipped into the barn one day in the 1920s, but not to pitch hay. They had it in mind to pitch woo.

Marie's mother spotted them from the kitchen window. She fretted for a while, then decided to investigate.

"*Mon Dieu!*" she gasped when she entered the barn. There, on the floor, was her darling daughter, writhing in ecstasy with that no-good Pierre.

The lady grabbed a broom and rushed forward.

"Stop! Stop!" she shouted, in vain. She raised the broom and crashed it down on Pierre's pulsating butt. Pierre made a couple of hasty exits.

Nine months later, Marie had a baby. She felt mortified. So did her parents. Marie and Pierre were the talk of town and country.

Pierre was told he would have to support the child. He refused. Marie sued Pierre for a declaration that he was the father of the child. She also sought an order for support.

The case was heard in the village of St. Paul de Metis, Alberta, about one hundred miles northeast of Edmonton. People came from near and far. The courtroom was packed long before District Court Judge Lucien Dubuc arrived to adjudicate the matter.

When he had heard all the testimony Judge Dubuc addressed the eager throng. This is what he said, as I got it from a Calgary writer, Susie Sparks, and a retired court reporter who got it from his father, the court reporter who took down the evidence and the judgement at the trial:

"Now we come to de time to sum up de evidence. Pierre, he come on to de farm as de hired man. Marie is de daughter of de farmer and Pierre, he become enamoured of her. One day he ask her to go to de barn. But he don't know that de maman watch dem from de window.

De maman, she tink, 'Ah ha, dere's somethin' funny goin' on here!' So she go out to de barn.

"De maman walk into de barn and see dem engaged in amorous delights. She pick up de broom and, just at de moment critical, she hit Pierre over de harse wit de broom.

"I don't tink dis boy is de fadder of de child. I tink de *maman* is de fadder of de child!"

This country teems with offbeat stories like that, weird and wonderful tales that are, for the most part, known only locally. Many of them deserve a national, nay, an international audience.

In pioneer times, when vast tracts of lands were opening up to settlement and legal talent was hard to come by, Western Canada abounded with wacky court decisions. Men with little education were appointed magistrates and justices of the peace and were expected to resolve complicated matters. In many cases they were hopelessly out of their league, but they unwittingly supplied us with plenty of laughs.

Back about 1890, for example, a justice of the peace in the Regina area pondered the case of a man who admitted taking a rowboat without the owner's permission. The owner said he wanted the fellow punished to the limit.

The JP had to decide what to charge the culprit with, so he started thumbing the index to his trusty Criminal Code. He looked under "boat" and it said "see ship." He turned to "ship" and it said "see piracy." Then he looked under "piracy" and it referred him to a section that said that stealing a ship amounted to "piracy." It also referred him to a section that said that the punishment for piracy – the *only* punishment – was death.

Undaunted, the JP drew up a charge of piracy. He asked the accused how he wished to plead to the charge and he said "guilty." The justice heard the evidence of the owner of the boat, then he imposed sentence:

"The sentence of this court is that you be hanged by the neck until you are dead, and may the Lord have mercy on your soul."

Immediately, the conscientious JP wrote to the Department of Justice in Ottawa and asked that the official hangman be sent to the scene of the crime as soon as possible. In the meantime, he ordered that the gallows be constructed so that they'd be ready for the hangman when he arrived.

It occurred to the Minister of Justice that the justice of the peace exceeded his jurisdiction, for capital offences were required to be tried by a judge and jury. The case was brought before a higher court for review and the JP's judgement was quashed. The gallows were never completed and the hangman never showed up. Neither did the prisoner. He broke out of the flimsy local lockup and fled as far and as fast as he could.

In an 1889 case, in the Northwest Territories, two justices of the peace swore out an information against a cow on a charge of being diseased, then tried the animal, found it guilty and sentenced it to die. (I kid you not. You could look it up: (1890), 1 *Western Law Times* 85.)

Morris Shumiatcher, Q.C., of Regina, tells about Judge C.B. Rouleau of the Northwest Territories who, back around the turn of the century, found a man guilty of pickpocketing.

"Charlie," he said, "I'm sentencing you to six months in jail."

"Oh, that's terrible," the man said.

"I want you to know," the judge continued, "that if I *really* thought you were guilty I would have given you six years."

On another occasion, Judge Rouleau bumped into a judge of the Court of Appeal, who told him, "I'm sorry, Judge Rouleau, but we had to overturn yet another of your decisions. If this continues, we'll lose confidence in your judgements."

"Don't let it worry you," he replied. "I lost confidence in the Court of Appeal a long time ago."

Many of the early western JPs and magistrates, especially those who lacked legal training, got horribly hung up on the doctrine of reasonable doubt. It's an ancient and sacred principle of criminal law that if there's a reasonable doubt it must be resolved in favour of the accused. If such doubt exists in respect of any essential ingredient of an offence, or upon the evidence as a whole, the accused is *entitled* to be acquitted.

It was well-nigh impossible to get that notion into the heads of many of our early judges. (Come to think of it, some of today's judges have a lot of trouble with it, too.) One judge used to say that whenever he felt the accused might be entitled to the benefit of the doubt, he'd lean back, close his eyes and wait quietly until the feeling passed before continuing with the case.

Some magistrates and JPs applied the reasonable-doubt rule *after* finding the accused guilty, like the magistrate who told the accused: "I find you guilty and I'm imposing a light sentence, a fine of twenty-five dollars, because I've had real doubts about your guilt."

Early in this century, in a small town in rural Manitoba, a farmer was charged with stealing thirty-five dollars from his neighbour. He was tried by two justices of the peace, which was the custom in those days.

The case took two days to try. One JP wanted to acquit the accused. The other felt he was guilty. They compromised and gave this judgement:

"The charge against the accused is dismissed – on condition that he return the thirty-five dollars."

Toronto lawyer Claude Thomson, Q.C., President of the Canadian Bar Association, tells a similar story of a popular Manitoba man who was charged, many years back, with stealing a horse:

"The trial was brief and when the jury returned with its verdict, the foreman stood and said, 'We find the accused not guilty, but he should return the horse.'

"The judge said, 'I cannot accept that verdict. If he stole the horse, it is your duty to find him guilty.'

"So, the jury retired and came back and the foreman again stood and he said, 'We find the accused guilty, but he can keep the horse.'"

Horse-stealing was prevalent in the early west and since a horse was often vital to a man's very existence, a stiff jail term always awaited the transgressor. Serge Kujawa, Q.C., of Regina, tells about a Saskatchewan judge at the turn of the century who sentenced a man to two years for stealing a horse. The accused was furious because the man ahead of him had been convicted of manslaughter and sentenced to only one year.

"How come he kills a man and gets a year and I steal a horse and get two years?" he asked the judge.

Without batting an eye, the judge replied, "There are some people who need killing. There are no horses that need stealing."

One of the most vivid judicial personalities in the early days of the Canadian West was Judge Joseph Camillien Noel, a kindly, courtly man who tried cases in northern Alberta from 1907 to 1920. In the Peace River country, he once tried a homesteader who was charged with stealing a pig from his neighbour.

The homesteader had had a crop failure and he and his family were practically starving. His more affluent neighbour had just had a litter of pigs and one bitterly cold winter's night the homesteader slipped next door and helped himself to a piglet. He cooked it immediately and the family ate its first meat in ages.

It was an open and shut case for the Crown: there were tracks in the snow between both properties and police found the carcass of the piglet on the accused's property. When the evidence was all in and the lawyers had presented their arguments, Judge Noel fidgeted, scratched his head, sighed, then told the accused to stand up.

"I find you not guilty of de charge," the judge said, to the surprise of everyone in court.

"But, Your Honour," the Crown Attorney protested, "the Crown has proven its case beyond the slightest shadow of a doubt. How can you come to such a decision?"

Judge Noel smiled kindly and said, "But, Mr. –, it was such a *leetle* pig!"

In this day and age, when there's such a glut of lawyers in Canada, it's hard to believe that there used to be a tremendous shortage of them. But there was, before the turn of the century and for many years thereafter – especially in the west. In 1884, there were only a few hundred people in Edmonton, and only two of them were practising lawyers. In 1890, Regina had been the capital of the Northwest Territories for less than a decade. It had 1,500 inhabitants, five or six of whom practised law. Calgary had about the same number of lawyers.

There were also very few judges. Two of the five judges of the Supreme Court of the Northwest Territories weren't lawyers. It was difficult to find anyone who had even a smattering of legal training. Hence the phenomenon of clueless JPs and magistrates. *Someone* had to do the work.

Lawyers could easily bamboozle these judicial babes in the woods. Bob Edwards, the brilliant owner and editor of the Calgary *Eye-Opener*, satirized the situation beautifully through a fictional lawyer, J.B. Cassidy, who appears to be a dead ringer for Edwards' pal, lawyer J.P. ("Paddy") Nolan.

Edwards tells us that Cassidy "was defending a man charged with stealing a hog and proceeded to hand out the following line of dope to the local justice of the peace:

" 'If Your Honour please, I would not for a moment mutilate the majesty of the law nor contravene the avoirdupois of the testimony, but I would ask you to focalize your five senses on the proposition I am about to propound to you.

" 'In all criminal cases there are three essential elements – the *locus in quo*, the *modus operandi* and the *corpus delecti*. In this case I think

I am safe in saying the *corpus delecti* and the *modus operandi* are all right, but there is an entire absence of the *locus in quo*. I therefore ask for a dismissal of the case.'

" 'I guess you're right,' said the J.P., who was not going to let the rubbernecks know that he had not the slightest idea of what Cassidy was talking about. 'Case dismissed.' "

Right on, Mr. Edwards!

One of the real-life Saskatchewan JPs was so clueless that when he was told that the next case to be tried was one of arson, he is reported to have replied:

"Arson? Arson? There are far too many sexual cases coming up these days!"

In the early 1900s, an untrained magistrate was conducting a preliminary hearing in a remote town in northern Alberta. The purpose of a preliminary hearing, of course, is to determine whether there's enough evidence against the accused to warrant putting him on trial. If the magistrate thinks the evidence falls short of this, he must discharge the accused and that's the end of the matter. If he orders a trial, *another* judge hears the case and decides whether or not the Crown has proven guilt beyond a reasonable doubt.

The magistrate hearing this case didn't know about this procedure, or had forgotten about it. Instead of committing the accused for trial, he found him guilty.

Counsel for the defence, the colourful Edmonton lawyer, Neil D. MacLean, was consumed with disbelief. Taking a leaf from his legendary colleague, Paddy Nolan, he said to the man on the bench, "Your Worship, I'm pretty sure that somewhere in the Criminal Code there's a section that says that in a situation like this the case should be set over for trial. Why don't we have a look at the Code?"

They flipped through the book for a while and then MacLean pretended to "find" the section. The magistrate saw the error of his ways, thanked MacLean for his kind assistance and said to the accused:

"Look, if I put your case over for trial you'll have to go into Edmonton and have a big trial in the Supreme Court. Your lawyer says you don't want all that trouble, and I don't blame you, so I'm dismissing this case right now." And he did.

This sort of loosey-goosey justice flabbergasted and frustrated knowledgeable people. City newspapers railed against it and said that only the legally trained should be allowed to preside in court. But reform was a long time coming and in the meantime the bungling, and the miscarriages of justice, rolled "merrily" on.

Not every magistrate and JP was a boob, of course. Quite a few were blessed with common sense and rendered decisions which were, for the most part, sound. But as the population increased and the laws became more complex, they too were often stumped as to how to decide cases.

Politics had much to do with the sorry situation. As a concerned citizen said in a letter to the Manitoba *Free Press*:

"Elsewhere in the world, untrained magistrates have always the advantage of professional assistance at the hands of the magistrate's clerk, who is always a lawyer of standing in his profession. Here, that is impossible. Again, through the miserable practice of each successive Government cancelling the whole commission and appointing their most violent political supporters . . . there is really no inducement to a man to wade through and master the musty volumes of Canadian and Manitoba statutes, for he knows how soon in the whirligig of politics his commission may be cancelled. Let men of the best standing and education be appointed in each district, and let the appointment be for life, during residence and good behaviour."

In 1895, in Manitoba at least, permanent "police magistrates" were appointed for most large municipalities, and they were paid a regular salary instead of having to rely entirely on court fees for their daily bread. They still lacked the advantage of legal training, though. It would be a long time before that shortcoming would be remedied.

Throughout the west, however, outside the towns and cities, the situation took a lot longer to improve. Geography was a big stumbling block, as it has been so often in our past. Distances between judicial centres were great. There were few judges, magistrates and lawyers to service these centres and just reaching them was tough enough indeed.

Itinerant servants of the law were gluttons for punishment. They travelled any way they could – by horse, ox car, stagecoach, riverboat. In later times, in certain areas, they could board a slow-moving train.

Before the construction of a second trans-continental railway, there was only the Canadian Pacific Railroad running east and west, with one branch to the north. When Regina lawyers wanted to attend court in Battleford, their first day's journey was made by train to Saskatoon – then little more than a few boardinghouses and a livery stable – and from there it was a two-day trip by stagecoach to Battleford.

Judge, lawyers and court officials often travelled together in what was called a "judicial party." When a judicial party set out for the far north, they'd be away from home for months. There was great camaraderie among them, but when they arrived in court they scrapped just as hard as they would back home.

Because of the distances and the dearth of legally trained individuals, inspectors in the Royal North West Mounted Police were permitted to serve as magistrates. In 1906, Bob Edwards criticized this practice in the Calgary *Eye-Opener*:

"Here we have a victim arrested by the police, prosecuted by the police, tried by the police and sentenced by the police. Technically the same man is arrester, prosecutor and judge. This may be all right (to a certain extent) in the lone north where there are no justices of the peace, but in populated sections the individual charged with a crime should be given a better show for his white alley.

"Happily, our Mounted Police Inspectors are men of character and possessed of a high sense of honour, and there never, to our knowledge, has been an example of arbitrary action on their part to the prejudice of a prisoner. But . . . it is hardly fair to compel a prisoner, who may be as innocent as Mary's little lamb, to take his chances before the bar of the very outfit that arrested him and procured the evidence against him."

Granted, that's not so hot. But it's mild compared with the caper pulled by Frank Cornish, a flamboyant character who certainly knew how to get his own way.

Francis Evans Cornish was a boisterous, charming rogue who was appointed Queen's Counsel at the tender age of twenty-six. Some years later, after leaving his native Ontario, he became Winnipeg's first elected mayor. He didn't win the mayoralty, really. He stole it. He received 383 votes, 175 of which were cast by obliging folks who voted twice. Cornish was the fellow who provided Winnipeg with its motto – "Commerce, Prudence, Industry." He stole it from the fine city of Hamilton, Ontario.

As mayor, Cornish was also a magistrate. One day he had to try himself on a charge of being drunk in public. He convicted himself, reprimanded himself and fined himself five dollars and costs. Then he helped himself, stating for the record: "Francis Evans Cornish, taking into consideration past good behaviour, your fine is remitted."

Two years later, when Cornish was no longer a member of council, he and some confederates raided a polling division. They blew out the lamps, knocked over the stove and fled with some election records. He was fined twenty dollars. This time he didn't have a friend in court. He had to cough up.

Another colourful lawyer from Winnipeg's colourful past was T.D. Cumberland who one day in 1893 was examining a witness in the County Court when a spectator called him a liar.

Cumberland wheeled around and said, "What was that you called me?"

"A liar!" the man replied.

Cumberland walked over and belted the fellow in the face, then returned to his place and apologized to the judge for losing his temper. The judge accepted Cumberland's apology and fined the spectator ten dollars for contempt of court. A few months later, Cumberland was appointed a County Court judge.

Ah, the wild and woolly west!

Frontier judges dispensed justice in a rough-and-ready way. They'd stick it to a horse thief, a rustler or a killer, but smaller fry were often treated with indulgence. The *Eye-Opener's* Bob Edwards recorded this example:

Magistrate Tom Burns had a tough case last week when an old drinking pal of his appeared before the Bench charged with drunkenness in a public place. The accused pleaded guilty.

Said Magistrate Burns, "I'll have to fine you seven dollars."

"Can't pay it," replied the prisoner.

"How about five dollars? Can you pay that?"

"No, Your Honour."

"I'll make the fine two-and-a-half then," said the magistrate. "Can you manage that?"

"Your Honour, I'm broke," confessed the unfortunate fellow.

"And dry, too, no doubt?" asked the cadi.

"Yes, Your Honour."

"Well," said the man on the Bench, "get the hell out of here, and [producing a quarter] here's two bits for you for a wee snifter and don't come back again. Case dismissed."

In another case heard by a rural magistrate, the question was whether a bottle of confiscated home brew had been manufactured by the accused.

The magistrate said he knew how to settle the issue. "Give me that bottle," he told the court clerk. The clerk obliged.

The magistrate pulled the cork, took a swig and announced his verdict: "No, that's definitely not his stuff! I'd know his stuff anywhere!"

And now, as the sun sinks slowly in the west, it's time to saddle up and mosey on home. But, before we do, let's take one last look at yesteryear. There's one more fellow I want you to meet. He takes the cake.

Many years ago, in British Columbia, a magistrate who lacked legal training was hearing a criminal case. He was new on the job and until that day had never had a lawyer appear in his court before.

A policeman, the only witness for the Crown, gave the evidence against the accused. When he was finished, the lawyer for the defence rose and said, "I submit that the Crown has failed to prove its case beyond a reasonable doubt, Your Worship, and I make a motion for dismissal of the charge."

The magistrate appeared bewildered. "There's a motion on the floor," he said to those assembled. "Is there a seconder?"

Defence counsel nudged his client.

"I second the motion," the accused declared.

The magistrate looked out at the audience and said, "All those in favour of the motion?"

Hands shot up all over the room.

"The motion is carried. Case dismissed!"

10

The Fastest Wit in the West

Back when the west was young, it used to be said that anyone contemplating the commission of a serious crime first ascertained the health of lawyer P.J. ("Paddy") Nolan, and the likelihood of his vigour continuing. Nolan's courtroom skills matched those of anyone anywhere and he was, to boot, the fastest wit in the west. Oh, he was fast!

"All the best criminals go to Paddy Nolan," wrote his friend Bob Edwards, editor of the famous Calgary newspaper, the *Eye-Opener*. They flocked to him because he won so many cases. And he won so many largely because of his wonderful sense of humour.

Patrick James Nolan, a big, friendly refugee from the Irish Bar who practised in Calgary from 1889 to 1913, had such a gift of the gab that it was said he could talk about a barber's pole and make an absorbing tale of it. Wit was the mightiest weapon in his arsenal of talents, and he used it repeatedly to squirm out of tight corners and to woo and win over the hearts and verdicts of judges and juries. By the time he was finished, he often had them in stitches.

"This keen-witted lawyer," Edwards wrote in 1907, "immediately proceeds to prove the entire innocence of his client, getting unfavourable witnesses all balled up so that they don't know their own names, playing on the jury box as if it were a jew's harp and finally pooh-poohing the prosecution into a condition of manifest imbecility. It has not infrequently occurred to us that it would be better for the sake of the country at large if P.J. was not so diabolically expert at his business."

After getting a man off on a horse-stealing charge, Paddy Nolan said to him, "Come clean now, Bill, you did steal that horse, didn't you?"

"Now look here, Mr. Nolan," the client said, "I always did think I stole that horse, but since I heard your speech to that there jury, I'll be doggoned if I ain't got my doubts about it."

Paddy's arch-rival, R.B. Bennett, who was an outstanding lawyer before he became Prime Minister of Canada, declared that Nolan was "the greatest jury lawyer I have ever known," high praise, indeed, considering the trouble Nolan had caused Bennett over the years.

Another Prime Minister, John Diefenbaker, loved to tell about a case in which Nolan demolished Bennett. Paddy defended members of a train crew of the Canadian Pacific Railroad who were charged with stealing a large quantity of goods from their employer. Bennett, as always in such cases, prosecuted for the C.P.R. He did a good job, too, and at the conclusion of his case things weren't exactly looking up for the accused. But Nolan suggested there was no case to meet. The judge agreed that the identification evidence left something to be desired, and he called upon Bennett for argument.

Bennett, decked out as usual in dark grey pinstriped pants and cutaway charcoal coat with a lace hankie dangling from the sleeve, had two young lawyers with him. Nolan, dressed in a nondescript suit and no hankie, had himself for company.

R.B. went into high gear. Turning to one of his juniors, he said, "Get me *Russell on Crimes* from the library!" The junior fetched him the book and he read chunks of it to the judge as he developed his argument. The judge said he still felt a bit uneasy about the identification evidence, so Bennett turned to the other junior and said, "Quick, get me *Phipson on Evidence!*" Bennett read selected passages and then wound up his argument. The judge was impressed. So was the jury.

The judge said that in view of the compelling argument he had just heard, he didn't think there was anything useful that Mr. Nolan could offer in rebuttal. "But I will listen to you," he said.

Paddy turned to an imaginary junior and, snapping his fingers, said, "Get me *Bennett on Bluff!*"

Pandemonium broke loose.

"The jury laughed for ten minutes," Mr. Diefenbaker said. "Paddy decided to put in no defence and the verdict was not guilty."

Retired Provincial Court Judge S. Tupper Bigelow, of Toronto, who used to practise law in Alberta, tells of another Nolan–Bennett encounter. In the early days of this century, when judicial officers were in short supply in the west, R.C.M.P. brass were sometimes permitted to act as magistrates. One such officer was Superintendent P.C.H. Primrose (who later was appointed a magistrate and after years on the Bench served as Lieutenant-Governor of Alberta). Bennett had a case that was scheduled to be heard by Primrose, and he decided to see him about it. He journeyed to Lethbridge and there, at the R.C.M.P. station, he saw a dirty-looking, poorly clothed man mowing the lawn.

"Is this the Primrose residence?" Bennett asked the man.

"It is."

"Well, my good man," he said condescendingly, "be good enough to tell the Superintendent I'd like to see him. My name is Bennett. R.B. Bennett, that is."

"What do you want to see him about?"

"I have a case before him tomorrow, if it's any of your business," Bennett said snottily.

"It certainly *is* my business," the man said. "I'm Superintendent Primrose, and if you want to discuss a case with me the place to do it is in open court, in the presence of counsel for the Crown. Good day, sir!"

The next day Bennett, still smarting from the rebuke, made an ass of himself. As he often did, he lost his temper and spoke arrogantly to the court. The magistrate kicked him out, telling him not to return until he'd learned how to conduct himself in a courtroom.

Now Bennett didn't drink – he thought alcohol was an abomination – but he often cut through the bar of the Calgary Hotel on his way to and from court. Upon his return from Lethbridge, he was taking this short-cut when he was spotted by Paddy Nolan, who was drinking with some of his cronies.

Nolan flagged him down and said, "You missed the Carswell salesman when you were out of town yesterday. He had a new textbook that he thought would interest you. He was very disappointed that he couldn't show it to you."

Bennett bit. "What book was that?" he asked.

"*Primrose on Ejectment!*" (There was such a book.)

In Moose Jaw, Paddy Nolan once defended a man charged with raping a young woman. Out of respect for Nolan's ability, the Crown brought in a formidable opponent, R.A. Bonnar of Winnipeg, to prosecute.

Bonnar led the girl through her evidence with great tact. Her story was simple, and it sounded convincing. She was a dairy maid, working on a farm, and she said that when she was returning from the barn with a pail of milk the accused jumped out of hiding and sexually assaulted her.

Nolan's famous cross-examination of the girl is a model of brevity and wit:

"How much milk were you carrying?"

"A gallon."

"And what was the size of your pail?"

"It was a gallon pail."

"Did it have a lid or cover of any sort?"

"No, it had no cover."

"Your milk must have pretty well filled the pail?"

"It was filled to the brim."

"And when you arrived home after meeting the accused, how full was your pail then?"

"It was still filled to the brim."

"I have no further questions."

Nolan's address to the jury was short and snappy. "Gentlemen, this young woman says that she lost her virtue, but saved her milk. What do you think about it?"

"Not guilty" was what they thought.

Paddy Nolan, a big handsome man with a large moustache, was a legend long before he died. Stories about him circulated throughout Canada, the United States, and even abroad. "His remarkable skill as a barrister, his marvellous and never-failing wit, his pungency of criticism and his warmth of praise, have been known these many years," the Calgary *Herald* noted with pride. "Stories of him are told around the world, each one testifying to the breadth of his Irish humour."

A favourite Nolan yarn concerns a time he was late for court. His client, an excitable Irish woman, was to be tried on a serious criminal charge. Everyone was ready to proceed, but Paddy hadn't shown up yet. The judge knew where he was. "We will take a short recess," he announced, then whispered to the court clerk, "Slip over to the bar at the Calgary Hotel and tell Nolan we're waiting for him. And tell him to shake a leg!"

Court reconvened fifteen minutes later – but still no Nolan. "All right," the judge said wearily, "arraign the accused."

The clerk asked her how she pleaded to the charge, and she exclaimed, "I'm not guilty, and with the help of my Lord God Almighty, my Saviour Jesus Christ, the Holy Virgin Mary and my lawyer, Paddy Nolan, I'll prove it!"

As she spoke, Nolan strolled into the courtroom and said, "In the absence of senior counsel, I'm ready to proceed."

In those days, when most magistrates lacked legal education, Paddy found it easy – and a lot of fun – to bamboozle them. In those days, too, racial remarks were much more common and socially acceptable to boot.

A client of his was caught stealing from a Chinese laundry. At the trial, Nolan repeatedly passed up opportunities to cross-examine Crown witnesses. Instead, he sat at the counsel table, flipping back and forth through his Criminal Code, a puzzled look on his face, as if something in the book had him stumped. He'd read, look up pensively, then shake his head. Once, he took the Code over to a window and studied it in a better light, but he still looked perplexed. The magistrate seemed intrigued by all of this.

Paddy called no evidence, then addressed the court:

"As Your Worship might have noticed, I've been having some trouble with the Criminal Code."

"Yes, I did notice, Mr. Nolan. What seems to be the problem?"

"Well, Your Worship, why don't you take your Criminal Code and look at it as I point out some things to you."

"All right."

"Now, there's theft under fifty dollars . . . "

"Yes, I see that."

"And theft over fifty dollars . . . "

"Yes."

"Theft of oysters . . . theft from the mail . . . theft of a testamentary instrument . . . theft of . . . "

"Yes, yes, but what is the problem?"

"Your Worship, there must be twenty different kinds of theft mentioned in this book. But nowhere . . . nowhere that I can see . . . is there anything whatsoever about theft from a Chinaman."

"Really?"

"Really."

Paddy became even bolder. "Your Worship, just in case I've missed something, let's you and I take another look. All right now, section . . . "

He took the magistrate on a guided tour of the Code.

"You're right, Mr. Nolan. Absolutely right. Where does that leave us?"

"Well, Your Worship, it's pretty simple. You can't convict the man. They caught him redhanded, but you can't convict him. You can only convict a person of something that's a crime, and it's not a crime if it's not in this book."

"Well, I'll be – "

"Now, Your Worship, this is obviously an oversight. Parliament must have *meant* to put 'theft from a Chinaman' in there, but they forgot. If it's any consolation, I'll tell the Minister of Justice about this and I'm sure that he'll see that this situation is fixed up soon."

Paddy "walked" his client – straight to the nearest saloon, where they laughed and laughed and laughed.

Nolan used his ingenuity again in the case of a poor widow who was charged with conducting a lottery. The woman had been left nearly penniless, and in order to raise a few dollars she tried to dispose of her husband's watch by a raffle. There was little chance of outright victory, but Paddy had an idea. He obtained a couple of raffle tickets and a few days before the case came on for determination he dropped in to chat with the judge who would be hearing the case. The judge knew nothing about the charge and hadn't learned yet that he would be trying a lottery case.

Paddy steered the conversation around to the subject of a widow he knew who was pitifully poor. He told the judge such a tale of woe about the woman that the judge, out of pure compassion, bought the two raffle tickets.

At the trial, the charge was clearly proven. Nolan aimed his argument directly at the judge's heart.

"Your Honour knows full well," he said, "the danger of these lotteries, and how even the best-intentioned people in the community fall victim to them and out of sheer sympathy for their object commit offences by buying tickets in them, as no doubt Your Honour has done on occasion yourself."

Nolan's audacity had paid off again. The widow received only a suspended sentence.

In another case, he represented a Fort Macleod man who'd been charged, in effect, with drinking out of season. The man had been "interdicted" – prohibited from buying or consuming alcohol – and had been arrested halfway through a bottle of whiskey. Again, there seemed nothing on which to base a defence. But Paddy prided himself on never quitting and – presto! – he came up with another dandy ploy.

As the case neared an end, he asked if any responsible person had definitely determined the contents of the bottle. No one had.

"Whiskey bottles have been known to contain some *strange* fluids," he declared. He suggested that the prosecutor sample the contents in the presence of the court. The prosecutor said this would be unethical, and he refused to do it.

Paddy then invited the magistrate to take a swig, but he also declined.

The magistrate suggested that since Mr. Nolan was somewhat of an expert on whiskey, he might conduct the experiment.

"Oh, no, Your Worship," he said. "When I consider what that bottle might contain, I wouldn't let it within a yard of my mouth."

The charge was dismissed for lack of evidence.

Patrick James Nolan was born in Limerick, in the south of Ireland, on, of all days, St. Patrick's Day, 1864. Being a lad of sunny disposition and sparkling good humour, he was known, almost from the start, as "Paddy." And that's the way it was for the rest of his fun-filled life.

He received his early schooling at Sacred Heart College in Limerick and completed his formal education at Dublin University, the Royal University of Ireland and the University of London. He was an honours graduate in classics from the Royal University. At Trinity College, Dublin, where he received his Bachelor of Arts and Bachelor of Laws degrees, he won a gold medal for oratory, no mean feat in a land where, it's been said, "all men are orators."

Eloquence was Paddy's long suit, and it was only natural that he should join the profession in which his great gifts of speech could be put to their best use. Called to the Irish Bar in 1885, he joined the famous Munster Circuit and practised for four years in the land of his birth, forging steadily, but restlessly, ahead.

He wasn't the content, stay-at-home type. He wanted to see some of the outside world. He got a hankering to go to Canada and did so when he was twenty-five. In 1889 he stepped off a train at Calgary, then a thriving, promising young town on the edge of a new frontier. He used to say that he had no idea why he chose Calgary, but it wasn't long before Paddy and the people of the district were glad that he did.

He was called to the Bar of the Northwest Territories in 1889, only the ninth lawyer to be admitted to practice in the vast, sprawling region from which, sixteen years later, would be created the provinces of Saskatchewan and Alberta.

For a while after his arrival, he was editor of the Calgary *Herald* – a good one, too, from all indications – and then he settled into the practice of law. In no time at all, clients were beating a path to his door.

People liked almost everything about him – his friendly disposition, his warmth and understanding, his magnetic personality and flashing wit. He had a lot going for him.

Winnipeg lawyer and writer Roy St. George Stubbs offered this assessment in 1939: "While he was by no means a profound lawyer, yet his readiness of wit and quickness of repartee, his infinite store of good spirits and his skill in introducing a note of humour or ridicule into the most serious situation, soon brought Paddy Nolan the reputation of being one of the most skillful advocates in the Northwest Territories. Before long he came to be looked upon as one of the institutions of the west."

Except for cases of libel and slander, breach of promise of marriage and damage claims for personal injuries, Nolan shied away from civil work. Criminal law was his first love, especially when a jury was involved.

Juries found him almost irresistible. He often had them laughing so hard they could scarcely follow the evidence – which was all right with him because he usually didn't want them wrapped up in the facts anyway. If they got serious, they might convict.

In the 1890s cattle rustling was rampant in the Northwest Territories, and rustlers usually turned to Nolan for skillful assistance in beating the rap. Few of his clients went down to defeat. So many rustlers escaped scot-free that the Stockman's Association, figuring that cattle thefts would continue unabated as long as Nolan was available for the defence, hired him as Special Prosecutor. Shortly thereafter, convictions became frequent.

On one occasion at Fort Macleod, Alberta, Paddy prosecuted a man on a charge of cattle stealing. He made out a very strong case against the accused but the judge said he had a "reasonable doubt" as to guilt and so he let the fellow off.

After the trial, Nolan took the northbound train for Calgary. Settling comfortably into his seat, he thought about the verdict, which he considered to be improper. Meanwhile, his well-filled valise protruded into the aisle. The judge took the same train and in passing down the aisle he stumbled over Paddy's valise. When he recovered his balance, he recognized Nolan and commented on the size of the baggage.

"It's full of reasonable doubts, Your Honour," Paddy said with a dig.

Nolan's heart wasn't in prosecuting and he soon went back where he belonged – on the other side of the fence, where *he* could look after the business of raising reasonable doubts.

Nolan was once returning to Calgary from Maple Creek, Saskatchewan, after the successful defence of a client charged with cattle theft. A man he met on the train complimented him on his handling of the trial and asked what fee he charged for a case of that sort.

"My friend," Paddy replied, "when I became a member of the great profession of which I am now such a noble ornament, I made a resolution, from which I have never since departed, to never take from any man more than he has." Yet he took some cases for no fee at all.

Nolan had another rule, which he followed all his life, and that was never to use his wit or any of his other talents to deliberately hurt another person – unless he was a rotten s.o.b. who really had it coming to him. He scrupulously avoided stepping on toes, and even when he destroyed someone on cross-examination, he almost always did it *nicely*.

Many of the people he "showed up" went to their graves bearing no resentment. "His sympathies were as tender as his body was big," one writer said. (And his body, it should be noted, tipped the scales at 275 pounds.) The man had virtually no enemies.

Paddy defended a man charged with stealing a steer from the ranch of W.R. Hull, a wealthy rancher whose property was situated near Claresholm, about seventy miles south of Calgary. Hull knew none of the facts of the case; he was called as a Crown witness simply to prove his ownership of the stolen animal. He was a self-made man who took great pride in his success and never passed up an opportunity to talk about himself.

There was no need to cross-examine Hull, but Nolan couldn't resist the temptation to try to get a rise out of him. He played with him gently:

"I believe you are one of the largest ranchers in Alberta, Mr. Hull?"

"Yes, Mr. Nolan, I believe I am."

"And where are your headquarters, Mr. Hull?"

"In Calgary, Mr. Nolan."

"And where are your hindquarters, Mr. Hull?"

Hull, thinking of his ranch, replied, "In Claresholm, Mr. Nolan."

"Well, if your headquarters are in Calgary and your hindquarters are in Claresholm, you certainly are the *largest* rancher in Alberta!"

Mr. Justice Milton Harradence, of the Alberta Court of Appeal, likes to tell about the time Nolan was consulted by a chicken farmer. The farmer had paid two hundred dollars for a highly pedigreed rooster, which was shipped to him by rail. When the bird arrived, one of its feet was missing. The farmer wanted to sue the railroad, and Paddy said he'd look into the matter.

"I have checked the law carefully, and in my opinion you don't have a case against the railroad," Nolan later told his client. "This is doubly unfortunate. You're out two hundred dollars and your cock's out a foot."

A thirsty policeman, visiting from Edmonton, once suggested that he and Paddy Nolan go to a bootlegger's for some refreshments. Nolan, who was on friendly terms with alcoholic beverages, said he knew just the place.

There was no one home at the house they went to, at 113 6th Avenue S.W., but Paddy said he knew where the whiskey was kept. When they'd had their drinks, the lawyer left a dollar bill on the kitchen table. The policeman followed suit.

The next day the policeman learned that the house they'd gone to was the residence of Patrick James Nolan, K.C.

Paddy was the first to admit that he was a little too fond of the grape. Towards the end of his career, he formed a partnership with a man named Eaton under the firm name of Nolan and Eaton. He once remarked that a better name for the firm would be Eatin' and Drinkin'.

In court, Nolan was once asked by the presiding judge how many oats he thought it would take to fill a certain bucket that had been brought into the case as an exhibit. "Your Honour," he quipped, "I don't know anything about dry measure."

The subject of drink also figured prominently in an imaginative political speech Paddy Nolan once made. For many years, Nolan and the Honourable Arthur L. Sifton occupied adjoining offices. Nolan appeared for the defence and Sifton for the prosecution in most of the important criminal trials in the Northwest Territories at the turn of the century, and though they fought each other ferociously in court, they were the best of friends out of court. Nolan was beaten the one and only time he ran for the Legislature, but he made numerous splendid stump speeches on behalf of others.

On this occasion, Paddy was campaigning on behalf of his old friend Sifton, then Minister of Public Works in the government of the Northwest Territories. Sifton's consituency contained several important mining centres, and miners did some pretty big-league drinking.

The trouble was that Sifton didn't imbibe at all. He was an ardent prohibitionist and he wouldn't even buy a drink for someone else. A candidate who hoped to win the miners' votes had to be "one of the boys." He had to belly up to the bar with his constituents and spring for a few rounds. If he didn't, he was dead in the water.

Nolan had another brain wave. Slipping into one of the mining towns a few hours ahead of Sifton, he gathered as many miners as he could into one of the saloons. After setting up a couple of rounds, Paddy addressed the throng:

"Boys, you know Sifton is to speak here tonight. He's a fine fellow but he has one fault that I fear may cost him a lot of votes. He's been dreaming of a night with the boys since the campaign began, but he doesn't know when to stop! I've had a hell of a time keeping him straight.

"If you boys will help, I think we can pull him through the meeting. I want you to see that no one asks him to take a drink, for if anyone asks him, he can't refuse. If he takes even one drink, God knows when he'll stop!"

The miners couldn't resist such an appeal and Sifton's meeting was a big success. In the election he captured most of the votes in that town. The old smoothie, P.J. Nolan, had proven once again that bullshit baffles brains.

Paddy Nolan was idolized by the younger lawyers. "To follow in his footsteps used to be the ambition of nearly every young lawyer of the west," Roy St. George Stubbs wrote. "To be junior to him in an important case was to have arrived in the legal profession. He never tried to hog the show. Large-hearted and free from envy, he would always go out of his way to give a junior an opportunity to show his mettle. When opposing a younger man, he never purposely embarrassed him. He would send his irresistible wit in other directions."

When Paddy Nolan was defending, the trial was never a tame affair. No matter how ordinary the charge might be, there was always a capacity house when Paddy entered the ring. The air would crackle with witticisms. Laughter would reign supreme.

In one trial, Nolan asked the judge to order all Crown witnesses to remain outside until called. Crown counsel asked that one witness, a member of the Calgary Bar, be allowed to remain in the courtroom. The witness was a tiny man, less than five feet in height. Paddy looked him over slowly, then turned to the court and said: "I have no objection, My Lord, to this witness remaining in the court, on the principle of the old legal maxim, *De Minimis non curat lex* – the law does not concern itself with trifles."

In 1907, Nolan was appointed King's Counsel, one of the first named in the new Province of Alberta. A few months later, when the University of Alberta was founded, he was appointed to the Board of Senators.

As an after-dinner speaker, Paddy had no peer. His addresses were, in the words of one writer, "rare soufflés of wit and whimsy."

At a dinner given in Calgary by Senator Pat Burns, one of the speakers described a trip which a party of newspapermen had made through Europe. He detailed the different countries which the group had visited, noting that they ended their junket by touring Austria-Hungary.

Then Paddy Nolan was asked to speak. Rising slowly from his chair, Paddy cast his eyes over the banquet table, which groaned under the weight of the sumptuous feast that had been spread upon it, and remarked: "These gentlemen may have gone through Austria hungry, but Pat Burns has evidently made up his mind that they will not go through Calgary hungry."

Nolan once attended a Knights of Columbus conference in New York, a city where his fame did not precede him. He was far down on the order paper, listed simply as "P.J. Nolan, K.C., delegate from Calgary," and he was asked to speak purely out of courtesy.

He was in top form, his wit razor-sharp and his fancy "soaring," one writer said, "on eagle's wings." When he finished speaking he received a wild ovation, and everyone wondered who this funny fellow was who had stolen the show.

Next day, newspapermen followed Nolan around New York and splashed his name and picture across the front pages of their papers. A New York *Sun* reporter rhapsodized for a column and a half about the brilliant barrister "P.J. Nolan, K.C., of Calgary – wherever that may be."

Stories about him continued to proliferate and in time he became a genuine, certified folk hero. Some of the tales are apocryphal; that's inevitable with folk heroes.

Bob Edwards told about the time Paddy Nolan was charged with the delicate task of informing a father that his son had been executed. The deceased was a remittance man – Calgary swarmed with such people – and his father was an English baronet.

With heavy heart, Paddy picked up his pen. He pondered the problem momentarily, then scribbled this note:

Paddy's platform gave way, too. He died from an internal hemorrhage on February 11, 1913, at the age of forty-eight. His son, Henry Grattan (Harry) Nolan, won a Rhodes Scholarship the following year, then went on to become an outstanding lawyer in Calgary. He was chief Canadian counsel at the Japanese War Crimes Trials and in 1956 he was appointed to the Supreme Court of Canada, the first Albertan ever to serve on our highest court. He died a few years later.

Legends fade fast when neglected. In 1939, when Paddy Nolan had been dead only twenty-six years, Roy St. George Stubbs lamented in the Canadian Bar Review that "a new generation has arisen that knows him not."

Sadly, that's even truer today, two further generations "removed." Hence this biography.

"Where are the Paddy Nolans of today?" Stubbs asked, away back in '39.

The answer is the same now as it was then: They're extinct.

11

A.B.

If you're looking for personalities with lightning-fast wit, you'll go a long way before you find the likes of A.B. MacGillivray.

"A.B.," as he was and still is affectionately known, was stipendiary (i.e., paid) magistrate for the Cape Breton, Nova Scotia town of Glace Bay from 1901 to 1941. Seven years before he secured that position, he was appointed stipendiary magistrate for the county in which Glace Bay is situated, and he continued in that post until he retired in 1941.

Today, forty-two years after his death, stories of the legendary A.B. MacGillivray still abound. He's a legend, the genuine article, and has been since the turn of the century. In Nova Scotia – especially Cape Breton – many people who have never had any contact with courts or "the Law" derive great pleasure from swapping MacGillivray yarns. Why, there are *children* in Cape Breton who can rattle off one "A.B." story after another!

I heard my first MacGillivray anecdote from my father when I was a lad of about sixteen. It goes as follows:

One morning, Magistrate MacGillivray looked down from the Bench towards the section of the court that was commonly called "the drunk tank." There he beheld a sad-looking array of men who'd lost their battle with booze, a miserable assemblage of shabby, smelly people waiting to be sentenced for being drunk in a public place.

There was one person in this group, though, who stood out from the others – a flashy fellow bedecked in blinding colours. He was a smart-ass, too, and A.B. couldn't stand people like that.

"Where did you come from?" the magistrate growled.

"Your Worship," replied the dandy, "this morning, just before breakfast, I slid down from Heaven on a rail."

A.B. shot back, "Well, I'm sentencing you to ninety days in the County

Jail for contempt of court. You can use the time to good advantage, pickin' the splinters out of your arse!"

Who was this man with the rapier tongue, this dispenser of justice who "reigned" for forty-seven years? Was he fair or unfair? Patient or impatient? Cruel or kind? Serious or comical? Loved or hated?

He was *all* these things, and then some. He was an individualist, the likes of which we rarely, if ever, see today. He was "different," for sure. He was, in the words of one of his biggest fans, "a character in every sense of the word."

Leo McIntyre, of Glace Bay, a recently retired Provincial Court Judge, is an enthusiastic student and an entertaining purveyor of the wit and wisdom of A.B. MacGillivray. In an article he wrote in 1952, Mr. McIntyre described "A.B." as follows:

"In his position as Magistrate, he was pledged to respect authority, yet he himself would be among the first to speak up at the abuse of it. His courtroom sessions were always well worth attending: they sparkled with his brilliant comment which to this day has provided us with a fund of humorous incidents still delightfully retold.

"Though he was not a practising barrister, as is required of magistrates today, he possessed a knowledge of law far beyond the ken of many learned counsel who pleaded cases in his court. Quiet-spoken, keen-witted, yet a master of the quick retort, he was slow to anger but quite severe when aroused. Being a farmer by birth, he was a man endowed with an abundance of common sense."

The Honourable J. Louis Dubinsky, of Halifax, practised law in Glace Bay from 1935 until his appointment to the Supreme Court of Nova Scotia in the 1960s. Now retired from that court but still active with the Federal Court of Canada, Judge Dubinsky tells a few MacGillivray anecdotes in his book, *In and Out of Court.*

"He was not a lawyer but he possessed a remarkably good ability to judge the facts in the ordinary type of cases that came before him," Judge Dubinsky said in a letter to me, adding that few of MacGillivray's decisions were appealed to higher courts. "The stories about him were legion. Most of these stories, I truly believe, were figments of the teller's imagination but were attributed to A.B. With every passing year, these stories grew and grew and A.B. became a legend which endures to this very day."

Apocryphal or not, many MacGillivray yarns are guaranteed to "lay 'em in the aisles." Take this one, for example, told by Donald A. Kerr, Q.C., of Halifax, who grew up in Glace Bay.

"Magistrate A.B. MacGillivray was conducting the preliminary hearing of a rape case arising out of an incident which allegedly took place in a second-rate boarding house in Glace Bay. The complainant set the scene: It was a muggy night, she said, and when she retired she left the hallway door open in hopes of inducing a breeze. She also cast aside the bedclothes. The accused, somewhat the worse for drink, apparently spied her through the open door and 'Before I woke up, he had it into me.'

" 'And how far did he have it into you, young lady?' A.B. gravely inquired.

"Mutely, the girl gestured with her hands, placing them about a foot apart.

" Woman,' A.B. said, 'there's only two of us in Cape Breton who can wake you up!' " Case dismissed.

And try this one on for size, also told by Don Kerr:

"A case of rape, or the attempt thereat, was being tried before Magistrate A.B. MacGillivray in Glace Bay. The accused, in his own defence, took the view that it would be unjust to convict him of the main offence because he had succeeded 'only a little tiny bit.'

" 'The issue, obviously, rests on the question of penetration,' said A.B.

" 'What's that?' asked the accused.

"A.B. explained in technical terms, but the accused remained bewildered.

" 'Look at it this way,' said A.B. 'I come to your house and knock on the door. You open the door but, seeing who it is, don't want to let me in, and you try to close the door on my head.

" 'Now, young man, I am not in the house by any means, but I can certainly spit a hell of a way down the hall.' "

MacGillivray's detractors – and he had plenty of them – objected to his salty language, among other things. He didn't pick and choose his words, not by a long shot. He called a spade a spade, probably because of his background.

Alexander Bernard MacGillivray was born in 1858 in the small farming village of Grand Narrows, Cape Breton, Nova Scotia, the eldest of six children of Augustine and Catherine MacGillivray. He received his formal education at the village school at Grand Narrows and from his parents. His father, who was a justice of the peace, was reputed to be a Gaelic scholar and A.B. "had the Gaelic" too. (In Cape Breton, people say that so-and-so "has" the Gaelic – not as in having a disease but as in having a gift.) A.B. spoke Gaelic fluently all his life, and peppered his courtroom utterances with Gaelic expressions.

Farming in those pioneer days didn't maintain the MacGillivray clan, so they departed for the then-developing industrial area of Cape Breton. At the age of thirteen we find A.B. in Glace Bay, working in the coal mines of that district. He worked hard, determined to acquire a thorough knowledge of all branches of the industry.

In 1882, MacGillivray married the former Mary Johnstone of Johnstown, Cape Breton, and they raised a family of seven children, one of whom, Augustine, or "Gus," as he was popularly known, later became Glace Bay's town solicitor.

In 1890, at the age of thirty-two, A.B. became Shipping Superintendent at Glace Bay harbour for the General Mining Company and in 1892 was appointed to the provincial board of examiners for the granting of certificates to mining officials. He continued in this job for many years, performing it in addition to his magisterial duties.

He received his first judicial appointment in 1894, at age thirty-six, when he got the nod as stipendiary magistrate for District 11, which included Glace Bay and the rest of Cape Breton County. In 1901, when Glace Bay incorporated as a town, he pulled some political strings and became the first stipendiary magistrate of that municipality, without having to relinquish the other position. The rest, as they say, is history.

Magistrate MacGillivray's "courtroom" was also his office. It was in a little one-room shack across the tracks from the town hall. A.B. presided over the town's "Police Court" from that dumpy building for almost all of his forty years on the job; towards the end of his tenure the court was moved into the town hall.

During his four decades of duty, His Worship rarely missed a day of work. "Despite his advanced age he was just as alert, both physically and mentally, as one half his age," the Glace Bay *Gazette* said in an obituary in 1943. "His decisions were regarded in all quarters as fair and just, and anyone appearing before him, regardless of whether they were represented by counsel or not, could be assured of a fair and honest hearing by the venerable stipendiary."

MacGillivray was an imposing man, about six feet two in height, erect and scholarly looking, with deep blue eyes and snow-white hair and beard, a Vandyke which he kept carefully trimmed. He took great pride in his appearance. He always wore a wing collar, and his heavy watch chain, worn over his ample vest, made him look like an elder statesman. He usually wore a steel-grey suit and derby, and his dapper appearance attracted much attention.

A.B. spoke in a strong Scottish brogue and, as reported by Judge Dubinsky, used a lot of Gaelic expressions: "It was never 'Yes' with him but always *'Yaish.'* His favorite greeting was *'Ciamar a tha sibh'* (*kemur u ha sheev*) – How are you? Another was: *'Tha 'n la math'* (*han laa ma*) – It's a good day. It was never 'thank you' but *'tapadh leat fhein'* (*tapu lat heyn*) – 'Thank you kindly.' "

MacGillivray's customary criticism of a talkative lawyer or witness was, "You're like the barber's cat – full of wind and piss." (An exception to this was his son Gus, who often appeared before A.B., though propriety dictated that he shouldn't. He usually spoke at length, without any parental disapproval, and the impression among lawyers, based on his win-loss record, was that Dad favoured Gus.)

A.B. had no court reporter and he painfully and slowly wrote down the evidence with a big fountain pen that was in almost constant motion. Once, as he paused to consider what a long-winded witness was saying, so he could sum it up concisely, a lawyer said, "I must take exception, Your Worship. You're not writing down all the evidence." MacGillivray pushed his glasses up on his forehead, leaned forward and snapped, "Young man, do you mean to say that you want me to write down all that bullshit?"

There's a punchline that's always attributed to A.B. MacGillivray, though there's evidence, reported elsewhere in this book, that someone else said it long before he did. To MacGillivray fans, that's inconceivable. They can't get enough of this story. So here it is, back by popular demand:

A.B. convicted a local smart-aleck on a charge laid by the town police.

"I'm fining you twenty-five dollars . . ."

"No problem, Your Worship, I've got that in me arse pocket."

" . . . and sentencing you to thirty days in the County Jail. Have you got *that* in your arse pocket?"

Sometimes things work the other way around and comical lines uttered by A.B. are attributed to someone else. I've seen this next punchline in a book about English humour, but Judge Dubinsky, who practised law for many years in Glace Bay and agrees that some MacGillivray yarns are suspect, says in his book that this one "truly belongs" to A.B.

First, the background: A young man was charged with having possession of stolen goods, knowing them to have been stolen, and he was to be tried by Magistrate MacGillivray. A friend told him that A.B. was known to be more lenient with a defendant who had no lawyer than with one who came to court with counsel, so he decided to plead his own case.

After the police testimony had been presented, the accused went into the box to explain how he came into possession of the stolen goods. He told the magistrate that he purchased the two tires, the radio and fishing gear, all of which had been found by the police in his home shortly after the theft, from a man he had known slightly. He said the man told him he needed money to go to hospital in Halifax and so was selling the stuff cheap. The accused swore he hadn't had the slightest suspicion that the goods were "hot."

When all the evidence was on record, A.B., in a kindly tone, asked the accused if he had "anything to say in summing up." The young man thought he'd detected a look of compassion on the magistrate's face and, encouraged by this, he leaped to his feet, raised his right hand upwards and, in a voice trembling with emotion, declared:

"As God is my judge, I am not guilty!"

A.B. lowered the boom:

"He's not! I am! And you are!"

A.B. MacGillivray respected the lawyers who appeared in his court, but he wasn't all that fond of them.

A senior lawyer, trying to discredit a Crown witness, unleashed a savage attack on the hapless man.

"How long have you been living in Glace Bay?"

"Oh, about thirty years now."

"Have you been living here continuously during that time?"

"Yes."

The lawyer moved in on his quarry.

"Are you sure you've been residing here continuously for all that time? Isn't it possible that you may have been away for a while?"

"I g-g-guess so, sir."

"What do you mean by 'I guess so'? You know perfectly well you were away for a couple of years in Dorchester Penitentiary. Isn't that true, witness?"

"Y-y-y-yes, sir."

A hush fell over A.B.'s crowded courtroom. All eyes were riveted on the lawyer as he jabbed the air with his finger and snarled:

"Now, tell His Worship *why* you were sent to Dorchester Penitentiary!"

The witness couldn't speak. He just stood there, staring at the lawyer. The lawyer moved in for the kill, his finger still jabbing, and when his face was almost pressed against the other man's face he hissed, "I want the truth, witness! Tell us why you were sentenced to the penitentiary!"

The witness remained mute. His terrified gaze turned from his tormentor to the magistrate and then to his wife, who sat in agony in the front row of the courtroom. He moistened his lips, as if he were going to say something, but no sound emerged.

Magistrate MacGillivray lifted his head from the long tablet on which he had been laboriously recording all the evidence. Slowly he put down his big fountain pen and, with blue eyes blazing and voice dripping with icewater, he snapped:

"He's not going to say anything. He doesn't have to. I remember very well why he went to the pen. He made the damned foolish mistake of having you as his lawyer!"

Another time, A.B. told a lawyer who'd been rambling on about sociological matters instead of focussing on the facts of the case: "Why, you're not a lawyer! You're nothing but a bloody philosopher."

The first time Judge Dubinsky appeared before Magistrate MacGillivray, he represented two young men who'd been charged with stealing twelve hens. After all the evidence was in, the young lawyer argued that although there were suspicious circumstances there was nothing to indicate the necessary "guilt beyond a reasonable doubt."

The counsel flogged that argument for all it was worth, and in so doing he lost track of time. Then he noticed that the magistrate was tugging at the gold chain which led to his vest pocket, so he thought he'd better skid to a halt.

"Your Worship," he said, "I hope I haven't taken up too much of your time."

A.B. pulled out his gold watch, glanced at it and said, "Well, I'm not going to stop you. You can talk as long as you want. But I think you'd better know something. The longer you keep me from my dinner, the longer will those tramps roast in the County Jail."

The rookie lost his first case and as his clients were led off to serve three months one of them whispered to him, "I don't know when we'll ever be able to pay you, but if you want to take something on account I can tell you where there are eight fat hens."

Leo MacIntyre tells of another instance of MacGillivray skewering a lawyer, but good!

A.B. and a friend were enjoying a few illegal "snorts" – and much happy conversation – in the parlour car of a train they were travelling in from Halifax to Sydney. A.B.'s friend went to the washroom and while he was gone an attorney from Boston introduced himself to MacGillivray and almost immediately launched into a denunciation of Canadians, who he said were nowhere near as industrious as Americans. "Why, before you people are up in the morning," he declared, "we have half a day's work done."

Just then, A.B.'s friend returned from the washroom, and A.B. introduced them. "I'd like you to meet Mr. So-and-so. He's a lawyer from Boston. His friends call him Mr. Exlax – because he works while we sleep."

Magistrate MacGillivray wasn't always witty. He could be mean and vicious and foulmouthed – and often was.

A Cape Breton lawyer who hasn't too many fond memories of the man recalls the time he appeared before A.B. in a paternity case. His client was a young man with a Russian-sounding name; let's call him Petrovitch. It was alleged that he was the father of twins born to a local lass with a Scottish name; let's say it was MacAskill.

The man denied paternity, and with that, before the evidence had even been heard, Magistrate MacGillivray thundered: "Petrovitch, you Russian bastard! If there's going to be any screwing of our Scottish girls in this town, there are enough of our own Scots around here to do it! Petrovitches have no right to go around screwing MacAskill girls!"

Guess who won the case.

This disgraceful tirade came from a man who prided himself on the decades of work he had done on behalf of his town, his parish and the Scottish Catholic Society. It's easy to see why many people, though they often laughed at his remarks, feared A.B. and, deep down, loathed him.

But enough of this negative talk.

Judge Dubinsky recalls a "delightful" time when he represented a merchant who had been brought before A.B. for violation of a town health regulation. After due consideration, it was decided that the best bet was to plead guilty and go for a reduced penalty. A.B., who was always on the verge of terminal writer's cramp, was relieved that he could lay down his hefty pen and relax. After hearing the "pitch" he imposed a light fine – $40.00 and court costs of $2.50.

On behalf of his client, Mr. Dubinsky handed the magistrate four $10.00 bills and a $5.00 bill.

A.B. had no cash box or anything of the sort. It was his custom to stick fines into one pocket of his pants and extract change from the other. He followed the same routine this time, but instead of forking over change of $2.50 he handed back a dollar more than that.

The lawyer handed the bill back and said, "Here's a dollar for you to put in the collection box next Sunday." A.B. said that was kind of him but it really wasn't necessary, and he passed the buck back again. Mr. Dubinsky rerouted the note once again and said, "Your Worship, you gave me too much change. The money really belongs to you."

"Jesus Christ!" A.B. said with a laugh. "I've been here a long, long time and I've seen all sorts of things happen in this courtroom. But never before have I seen a Scotsman give too much money to a Jew – and the Jew give it back to him!"

Another light-hearted story concerns a time that he allegedly ran afoul of the law. It is said that early in the century A.B. and a fellow magistrate, having each acquired one of those new-fangled "automobiles," decided to try out their machines on the highway between Glace Bay and Sydney. Merrily they rolled along, driving as fast as they could, passing each other, cutting in on each other and just generally having a grand time with their new toys.

Their fun was rudely interrupted by a policeman who charged them both with speeding. Since both accused were magistrates, they decided to try each other.

Magistrates didn't wear gowns in those days but MacGillivray and his friend decided that they should be gowned for such a solemn occasion as their own trials. So they borrowed a gown from a choirmaster, then repaired to A.B.'s courtroom.

MacGillivray was the first to be tried. The policeman presented the evidence against him and then the presiding magistrate asked A.B. if he had anything he wished to say in mitigation of sentence.

A.B. was eloquent in his own behalf. He said he was very sorry he had broken the law but he'd never had a new car before and he doubted that he'd ever be buying another one, so it was highly unlikely that he'd ever be tempted to show off again. He assured the court that never again would he commit a driving offence.

The man on the bench said he was very impressed by A.B.'s argument, and fined him only five dollars.

Court adjourned briefly while the men switched roles and MacGillivray slipped into the gown. Then court reconvened.

The policeman testified again and the accused gave the same "pitch" that MacGillivray had given earlier.

"This is a very serious offence," A.B. began ominously. "There's too much of this sort of thing going on lately. People are getting hurt in these new machines. One of these days someone is going to get killed. Why, this is the second such case this court has heard this morning. I've got to make an example of you – one hundred dollars and costs!"

An oft-told story about MacGillivray concerns the time a vaudeville show, with dancing girls in rather skimpy costumes, came to Glace Bay. The good citizens of the town raised quite a fuss about the show and the local priest, Father MacAdam, denounced it from the pulpit.

To determine whether or not the show exceeded the moral standards of the day, it was decided that a committee of two should see the show and report its decision. The committee consisted of A.B. and a longtime stalwart of the church, Neil J. Gillis. Off they went to the Savoy Theatre to do their duty.

The next morning, Mrs. MacGillivray, who, for purposes of ready identification, was known locally as "Mary A.B.," was talking with her neighbour, Mrs. Gillis, about the visit of their husbands to the Savoy.

"What did A.B. think of that show last night?" Mrs. Gillis asked.

"I haven't had a chance to discuss it with him yet," she replied, "but I'm pretty sure he was dead against it."

"What makes you say that?"

"Well, when they came home last night I overheard them talking about one of the dancers and A.B. said a couple of times, 'Neil J., wouldn't you like to take a whack at that one?' "

Alexander Bernard MacGillivray continued to enjoy good health for two years after his retirement from the Bench in 1941, then died a few days after suffering a stroke. He was slightly shy of his eighty-fifth birthday. Mary A.B. died nine years before him.

Whenever Cape Bretoners get together to swap yarns – which will be often because it's one of their favourite pastimes and they're damn good at it – they'll tell tales of the wit and rollicking humour of A.B. MacGillivray. And while they're at it, they're sure to pay homage to Mary A.B., no slouch herself, by relating, for the zillionth time, this classic story:

A.B. left home one Friday afternoon to visit a sick friend in a nearby town. He said he'd be back that night, but he didn't return till Sunday night. When he weaved his way up the walk into the house, Mary A.B. was there to "greet" him.

"And where the hell have you been?" she asked sweetly.

He replied that he'd visited his friend and they'd had a long conversation and then other friends dropped by and they all got to talking at length and he decided he should stay and look after his friend for the weekend.

Then Mary A.B. noticed that her husband's coat and shirt bore rum and vomit stains.

"How did this happen, pray tell?"

A.B. "explained" that on his way home in the streetcar he had to stand because the seats were all taken and a drunk boarded the car and stood next to him, waving a bottle of rum and asking him, repeatedly, if he wanted a drink.

"And you declined, of course."

"That's right, my dear, I did. I told him to leave me alone, but he kept pestering me and waving that goddamn bottle around. The streetcar was lurching quite a bit and the sonavabitch spilled some rum on me. Then, when we got to Callaghan's Corner, he puked all over me."

Mary A.B. seemed to be giving him the benefit of the doubt, but he wasn't sure.

"What happened then?"

"Well, my dear, when we got to Senator's Corner I hauled him off the car and had him arrested. He'll be in the drunk tank tomorrow and I'm going to throw the book at him!"

"You be sure to, A.B.. That's awful, what he did to you."

A.B. was delighted. The missus seemed to have bought his story.

"Don't forget to throw the book at that fellow," she reminded him on his way to work the next morning.

"I will, I will, don't worry."

A.B. was busy sentencing drunks when the phone rang in his office-courtroom. It was his wife calling.

"Have you thrown the book at that guy yet?"

"Not yet, dear. But he'll be in front of me in a few minutes. Why did you call? You know I don't like getting telephone calls when I'm in court."

"I just wanted to tell you that you'd better throw the book extra hard."

"Why do you say that, my dear?"

"Well, I've just been looking at your clothes again and it turns out that the bugger also shit in your pants!"

12

"Justice –
With Costs"

George Theophilis Bradfield Walsh, Justice of the Supreme Court of Ontario, was pleased with how things were going. During his stay in the county town of Lindsay he had presided over a number of serious criminal and civil cases. With the "heavy" stuff out of the way, he began to relax. There were a number of divorce cases to try and then his decks would be cleared and he'd be on his way to his next assignment. He didn't mind divorce cases, as many judges did. In fact, he enjoyed them.

Entering the courthouse for the start of another day's work, walking quickly and jauntily as he always did, His Lordship thought he'd say hello to the lawyers who were donning their court gear.

He stood in the doorway of the barristers' robing room – all five feet, three inches of him – and declared to all assembled: "Today, boys, is *fun* day!"

Every day was fun day for George Walsh, a comical little man who looked like he'd just stepped out of a Charles Dickens novel. He loved life, he loved people, and most of all, he loved the profession of law. Almost everything about it interested him, especially court work, which was the centre of his existence for nearly half a century.

He was an outstanding lawyer and a very unusual judge. He was a little man but a big star, highly respected by lawyers and by most judges. The people who worked in and around the courts loved him and appreciated him – oh, how they appreciated him! – because he was a "character," a ray of sunshine in the usually-dreary courts. He brightened their lives. He did it with humour and he got away with things that no one else could even dream of getting away with. He had a "touch."

In Ontario, we were lucky enough to have him around for forty-nine years – from 1913 to 1962. When he died, they immediately broke the mold and tossed it into Toronto Harbour. It's highly unlikely we'll ever see his like again.

When I let word escape that I was writing this book, lawyers, judges, and others too, immediately let it be known that they hoped I'd tell "lots of George Walsh stories." They can't get their fill of George. Many laugh at the mere mention of his name.

"George Walsh was a born comedian," says Ralph S. Mills, Q.C., who is now in his early eighties, looks ten years younger, and still practises law in downtown Toronto. "George also had a photographic memory. You could hand him a three-page document he'd never seen before; he'd scan it briefly and hand it back, memorized."

The comedic ability Mr. Mills refers to punctured the pomposity of a number of judges – the Ontario Court of Appeal in particular – and led to many a victory for the wily and witty Walsh, who hated pretension and affectation.

In the thirties, he was in the Court of Appeal almost every day. He was one of the few lawyers who could function in the hostile environment of the court back then, when arrogant, cranky judges constantly badgered and bullied lawyers who dared to venture into their midst. "The Terrible Five," as the nucleus of the court was known, often reduced grown men to tears. Many a promising forensic career was nipped in the bud when lawyers, unwilling to suffer the slings and arrows of outrageous judicial conduct, swore off court work and confined themselves to their offices. They, and many others who declined to be martyrs, sent mounds of cases to Walsh to be argued on their behalf. "Let George do it" was their motto.

And George did it, with a lot of hard work and the light touch he could summon up instantly whenever he thought it would come in handy.

One afternoon, as he started to wade into his third appeal of the day, Walsh was interrupted by one of the judges, who asked: "Mr. Walsh, do you appeal *all* your cases?"

"No, My Lord," he shot back, "only the ones I lose."

A slight smile loosened the corners of the judge's mouth.

And as time went on, slight smiles became full-fledged smiles, chuckles, and, on rare occasions, guffaws. He was starting to get somewhere with these curmudgeons. They were showing unmistakable signs that they enjoyed having him aboard – especially when he spoke on the crucial subject of costs.

Ah, costs! For centuries, this has been the good news-bad news message at the end of court cases, the "spoils" that warm the heart of one party and pierce the heart of the other. Generally speaking, "to the victor go the spoils." But not always. The court has discretion in the matter. It can deprive a winner of costs, perhaps because it disapproves of the way he acted. In addition to paying the full cost of his own lawyer's services, the contestant who is tagged with "party and party" costs must pay a goodly portion of his opponent's expense. But it can be even worse than that: if the court, exercising its discretion, orders him to pay "solicitor and client" costs, he ends up paying practically the entire bill for both sides of the battle. No wonder lawyers go into high gear when the subject of costs comes up for debate.

Many of Walsh's witticisms arose out of such debates. In a contested-will case, for example, the judge rejected the claim that the will was invalid and said that, having regard to all the circumstances, he was making no order as to costs. George Walsh, who represented the executor of the estate, asked hopefully, "But there will be costs to the executor, Your Honour?"

"No, Mr. Walsh, I said no costs to anyone."

To which Walsh replied, "Oh, Your Honour, it's plain to see that this testator died in vain."

One momentous day, a judge asked Walsh what he was seeking for his client and, without batting an eye, he answered with the words that gained him fame: "Justice – with costs." That became his rallying cry, and many lawyers wished they'd said it first.

His friend, Mr. Justice Willard ("Bud") Estey, of the Supreme Court of Canada, tells the story of another famous Walshian witticism:

"One day in Surrogate court, George was responding to an attack from the Bench for the endless motions and interlocutory proceedings brought in the administration of the estate then before the court, and particularly the interpretative question being posed by Mr. Walsh on that occasion, to which George responded in his usual head-shaking loud and serious way:

" 'This is an important question, and while it is true that the legal expense attendant upon the resolution of the money issues in this estate has been great, let us not forget that the assets of these great estates should never be frittered away on the beneficiaries.' "

In a case Walsh won in the Supreme Court of Canada, the main judgement of the court was written by his old friend, Mr. Justice John Cartwright. It was a learned and literary judgement and, as usual, the last paragraph dealt with costs, which were awarded to George's client.

A few days later, Mr. Justice Cartwright saw Walsh on the street and, fishing for a compliment, asked: "What did you think of my judgement, George?"

"I don't really know, Johnny," Walsh replied. "I haven't read it all yet – but the last paragraph is good."

"Wit sometimes enables us to act rudely with impunity," a chap named Duc de La Rochefoucauld observed back in the 1600s. Aristotle noted that "wit is cultured insolence." They must have had a sneak preview of George Walsh.

In the thirties, he appeared in the Ontario Court of Appeal in a case pertaining to a separation agreement. A man making low wages had agreed in writing to pay his wife twenty-five dollars a month. His fortunes improved tremendously and now, even with a depression raging around him, he was hauling down about $80,000 a year. His wife thought this was kind of unfair and she sued for a raise. The trial judge said she was bound by what she had agreed to in writing. She then took the case "upstairs."

The day the case came on for argument, the lady's lawyer was facing Mr. Justice William Renwick Riddell, Mr. Justice Cornelius Arthur Masten and Mr. Justice Robert Grant Fisher – three-fifths of "the Terrible Five" – and his opponent was George Theophilis Walsh. Sitting nearby was Walsh's law student, John A. Deacon, who these days serves on the Provincial Court (Criminal Division) in Brockville, Ontario.

Walsh's argument was, in effect, that the lady was bound by the agreement, her husband had never missed a twenty-five-dollar payment and was quite content to keep making the said payment, and that was all there was to it.

Mr. Justice Fisher leaned over the bench and quavered, "Oh, Mr. Walsh, would you ask your wife to live on twenty-five dollars a month?"

Walsh sniffed back, "I'd prefer if Your Lordship asked her."

Judge Deacon says he thought Walsh's goose was cooked when he was asked the question. "But, just like that, he came up with that great reply."

George Walsh was born in Millbrook, Ontario, in 1890, and received his early schooling there. He planned to be a druggist but he became interested in law, and fresh out of high school, he entered his articles of law with a Millbrook lawyer. In 1910 he entered Osgoode Hall Law School in Toronto and for his three years he ranked fourth in his class.

It was a class that produced two Chief Justices of Ontario, a judge of the Supreme Court of Ontario, a large number of County Court judges and magistrates, and quite a few leading lawyers. From the day he started practice in 1913, he stuck pretty much to court work.

Walsh served in the First World War, enlisting as a private and emerging at war's end with the rank of adjutant in the 216th Battallion. It was known as "The Bantam Battallion" because no member was over five feet, six inches tall. Its emblem was a bantam rooster.

In some ways, that emblem fit George himself. He was extremely short and his egg-shaped head was almost totally bald. He was friendly and effervescent, always bustling with energy and cheerfulness. In later years he looked very much like Barry Fitzgerald. (When I first saw him I thought that Bing Crosby would show up at any minute and join him in singing "Tooralooraloora.") He walked quickly on bandy legs and he talked quickly, too. When he emphasized words he sort of snorted them. His voice was a little gravelly. His friend, Mr. Justice Estey, described it as "half W.C. Fields and half Andy Devine."

There are *two* Mr. Justice George T. Walshes perched in the family tree. George Tucker Walsh, who practised law with his father for eight years, was appointed to the Supreme Court of Ontario in 1978. He says that someone once asked his father, "To what do you attribute your success?" and his Dad said, "to the fact that I look Jewish, have a Catholic name and go to the United Church." He got a lot of business from all three sectors.

In fact, George Walsh Sr. got a lot of business from *everywhere*. He was a very friendly, likeable, talented lawyer, and he worked extremely hard – twelve hours a day, six days a week was par for the course – much of his business coming from lawyers who didn't want to mix with the man-eating sharks on the Court of Appeal. He was a top-notch counsel and not a "clown," as some people who don't know much about him sometimes think. They mistake the humour for frivolity. Not so. It was an extra arrow in his quiver.

Walsh was a non-drinker who contributed generously to temperance organizations and to his church and various charities. He had no hobbies and he didn't play or watch any sports but he loved to gossip, a fact he freely admitted. He kept in close touch with who was doing what in the legal community, and the community at large. He spent his summer vacation each year at the same Muskoka resort, eating all his meals at the same table – "to gain gossip items," he told his friend Ralph Mills with a wink.

Walsh also loved to make money, which explains why his eyes lit up whenever the subject of costs arose. He made big money, even during the Depression, from a tiny, low-overhead office where there was scarcely enough room to swing a cat.

When Judge Deacon went to work for Walsh for two dollars a week, in 1936, he was amazed to see that the office of this man who was driven to and from work by a chauffeur had no pictures or diplomas hanging on the walls and no decor to speak of. "He played it poor," the former student says. The library consisted solely of the Revised Statutes of Ontario and the single-volume Rules of Practice. His boss had no need for the latter because he had the Rules memorized and, besides, he served on the Rules Committee of the Law Society.

"Deacon, my boy," the boss said, "when you've been with me for a while you'll appreciate that law is based ten percent on knowledge and ninety percent on bullshit. I have the ninety percent up in my little head, and the ten percent is in my library at home."

John J. Robinette, Q.C., confirms Walsh's play-it-poor approach. "I remember once going into his office, which was barren of any luxury," Mr. Robinette writes. "The floor was linoleum and the seats for the clients were wooden kitchen chairs. There were files all over the place and there was only one chair without a file on it. George explained I would have to sit on that one because some of the other chairs were his estates department."

I phoned one of the lawyers who worked for Walsh in the 1930s, figuring he'd have plenty of anecdotes about his former mentor. "I don't have any," he surprised me by saying. "He wasn't funny at the office."

Judge Deacon begs to differ. He recalls a time in the office when Walsh caught him reading a twenty-page salacious letter from a woman client who was involved in a steamy sex case. George, noticing that his student was enjoying the epistle, commented: "Deacon, you're just like me. You like anything that has the scent of fornication about it."

He had quite a way with words. Once, describing a cold-hearted judge, he noted, "His smile is just like the silver plate on a coffin." On another occasion, when his involvement in a case was about to end, he paid a sum of money into court and asked that he be allowed to siphon off his costs. Chief Justice H.E. Rose wouldn't allow this and after a prolonged discussion reminded him that his costs were perfectly safe because the money would be in court until the case had been resolved. Walsh, who wanted his money sooner rather than later, said in mock despair, "Oh, My Lord, that's just like offering a milk ticket to a starving baby!"

George Walsh fired off lines like these spontaneously. His son says his father never "researched" snappy comebacks, the way some people do. Repartee came naturally. "He had the nimbleness of mind that enabled him to come up with the appropriate comment," His Lordship told me. "He could always rise to the occasion."

He sure could. Walsh once appeared in the Court of Appeal in the morning and successfully argued a particular point of law. That afternoon there he was, at the same old stand, arguing the opposite way in another case. When one of the judges pointed out his dilemma, George replied without hesitation, "Well, My Lord, I've given the point much thought over the lunch hour and I've seen the error of my ways. I was hoping to convince Your Lordships likewise."

Another time, he was heading into the Court of Appeal with his arms full of books when he met a lawyer who was known, and hated, for his non-stop sarcasm.

"Mr. Walsh," the man said, "I thought you knew *all* the law! Why are you taking those books into court?"

"These aren't for me," he shot back. "They're for the judges."

On one of the rare occasions when he wasn't properly prepared, Walsh got himself nicely cornered in the Court of Appeal. The case hinged on the nature of a certain document and Chief Justice R.S. Robertson, who was presiding, persisted in asking him whether he was arguing that it was an option to purchase or an agreement to purchase. Walsh didn't want to take an immediate stand on this vital matter, so he hedged. The Chief Justice insisted on having a definite answer, and he asked him once again. Walsh, in desperation, quipped, "Whichever you prefer, Your Lordship, so long as I win!"

Walsh's practice continued to flourish over the years, and so did his popularity among judges, lawyers, law students and court personnel. He had a cheery, and usually humorous, greeting for everyone, and he always had time to stop and chat with students he encountered in and around Osgoode Hall Law School. Two of the students he trained in his office became Premiers of Ontario – Leslie Frost and John Robarts.

In 1929, Walsh was appointed King's Counsel and in 1951 he became a Life Bencher of the Law Society of Upper Canada – a rare distinction – by virtue of having been elected a Bencher by the profession in several of the elections that are held every four years. The Benchers are, in effect, a "board of directors" who run the profession in the province. Each time he ran for this prestigious post, he either topped the polls or came close. "My greatest satisfaction in life," he said later, "has been my duty as a Bencher and working on behalf of the students. My door is always open to them."

It continued to be open to fun, too, for the rest of his days.

Some of his best-known antics occurred in a case in which he appeared in St. Thomas, involving a young boy who had shot his companion while the two were out hunting rabbits. In his address to the jury, the irrepressible Walsh re-enacted the hunt. At one stage of his charade, when he was in mid-air, the trial judge exclaimed, "Stop, Mr. Walsh, stop! I don't understand what you are now portraying, and it may be that the jury doesn't either. At this point, are you the boy who was shot, or are you the boy who had the gun, or are you the rabbit?"

Judge Donald G.E. Thompson, of Barrie, Ontario, recalls fondly a divorce trial he attended in Toronto in the forties. Chief Justice H.E. Rose presided and George Walsh, who appeared for the plaintiff, sought to prove that the defendant had been served substitutionally through a court-approved advertisement in the Toronto *Star*.

Walsh came to court with a month's supply of the newspaper, between heavy board covers, and he held the big, cumbersome collection right up in front of the judge so that he could verify that the advertisement had been published. His view of the judge was blocked by the big production he was holding up, and his little arms were getting tired. After several minutes of this, George inquired sweetly, "What are you doing, My Lord, reading the funnies?"

Walsh had a lot of divorce cases in his day, both as a lawyer and as a judge, and every one of them had to do with adultery; in Ontario courts, it was the only ground for divorce until 1968.

Former Ontario Chief Justice G.A. Gale chuckles when he recalls the day George Walsh shuffled into the office of Helen Palen, the Assistant Registrar of the Supreme Court of Ontario who looked after motions, to file a motion concerning a divorce case, of course on the ground of adultery. "He put a fifty-cent stamp on the Notice of Motion and a ten-cent stamp on each of his affidavits," the former Chief Justice said. "When he finished, he said: 'Miss Palen, Miss Palen, do you realize that you are practically living off the avails?'"

The subject of adultery interested him greatly, judging from the large number of wisecracks he made about it in conversation, at the bar and on the Bench. His interest wasn't necessarily prurient; it might have been simply a recognition of the fact that adultery had been good to him. For one thing, it had made him a lot of money. For another, it was a sure-fire laugh-getter.

A Toronto lawyer met him at Osgoode Hall one day in the early forties and asked him, "How's business?" He replied, "Well, with gas rationing there are fewer cars on the road and so there's much less automobile negligence work. But, fortunately, adultery is rampant."

A court official once bumped into Walsh, gowned and ready for action, outside a Toronto courtroom where divorce cases were being heard.

"George!" he said with surprise. "You're supposed to be on vacation. How come you're in divorce court?"

"Where could I have more fun than here?" he asked as he swished into court.

George Walsh could have had fun picking his teeth! He was enthusiastic about almost everything, it seemed, and his good humour could chase away just about anyone's blues.

He always convulsed lawyers with laughter when he delivered his standard "lecture" on how he conducted a lawsuit. He said he'd "learn just enough about the facts not to get confused" and then he'd move on to the most important part of his preparation. "Yes, ladies and gentlemen," he'd say, "I'd reach for *the* book, yes, *theeeeee* book . . ." Then, from his vest pocket, he'd gleefully extract the tiny but crucially important Circuit Guide, which announced which judges were scheduled to sit in which communities on what dates.

In October, 1958, George Walsh learned that *his* name would soon be appearing in the Circuit Guide. He'd been appointed to the High Court of Justice, the trial division of the Supreme Court of Ontario. The day his appointment was announced, he met his former student, John Deacon, on the street. After Deacon had congratulated him, Walsh said modestly, "Don't worry about me, Johnny, I can dispense justice with the best of them."

The day *after* he became a Supreme Court judge, he bumped into George Johnston, Chief Librarian at Osgoode Hall.

"Why did you accept the appointment?" Johnston asked the new judge. "I thought you wanted to continue indefinitely as a leading counsel."

"Well, I'll tell you, George," His Lordship replied. "I've appeared in every small county town in Ontario as counsel, and whenever I've gone to the local hotel and asked for a room with a bath, I was always told: 'The

Supreme Court judge has it.' So I'm going back now to get those baths!"

Jake Dunlap says that George Walsh was one of the kindest men he's ever known. He recalls a divorce case in Ottawa in which the petitioner's lawyer talked on and on but got nowhere.

Many judges would have severely scolded the lawyer, but the presiding judge, Mr. Justice Walsh, inquired softly:

"Mr. –, do you have any evidence of adultery?"

"Oh, yes, My Lord," the lawyer said, "I've got oceans of it."

His Lordship replied, "Well, give me a little trickle, will you?"

Mr. Dunlap, a very funny man himself, says Walsh made wisecracks from the Bench "to put people at ease when they appeared before him." George Baker, who was Walsh's court reporter in many cases, agrees. "The comedy was a facade," he says. "He relaxed people, and disarmed them, with his humour. It was quite an asset."

One day, after hearing divorce cases all morning, His Lordship declared, "Court is adjourned until two p.m. – and let there be no adultery during the lunch hour!"

In one divorce case he presided over, the plaintiff and co-respondent were extremely attractive women. They testified, and so did the defendant husband, and to everyone's relief, His Lordship granted the decree.

When the husband was leaving the courtroom, the judge issued a stern command: "Witness, come back here!"

With trepidation, he returned towards the Bench.

His Lordship took another good look at the man's wife and girlfriend, then leaned over and said in a stage whisper, "Man, you sure have good taste!"

In a memorable contested divorce case, presided over by Mr. Justice Walsh, the plaintiff, the defendant and the co-respondent were all members of a religious sect and wore the traditional garb of their congregation – the man in a black suit, the women in long black dresses and shawls, their heads covered by bonnets. The witnesses, eight or ten men and women, also belonged to the sect and were dressed similarly.

When the trial was over and Mr. Justice Walsh was leaving the Bench, he was amused to note that all the participants were walking out of court together, almost in formation. He paused momentarily and, cupping his hands around his mouth, declared, in a loud, ringing voice, "Onward, Christian soldiers!"

In a real way, George Theophilis Bradfield Walsh was a Christian soldier himself. He certainly spread joy, as a good Christian is supposed to, and, without a doubt, he left the world a better place than it was when he arrived on the scene. He brought to a great many people what Sydney Harris calls "the incalculable gift of laughter." So he went a little overboard at times. It was all in fun.

Mr. Justice Walsh's mother, who made it into her nineties, shied away from going to church in her later years because she said she was afraid of dying there. Her son, trying to persuade her to go to services with him, used to tell her that church was "the best possible place to die."

On Sunday, September 30, 1962, George Walsh arrived at Timothy Eaton Memorial Church in Toronto, the church he had attended and contributed to generously for many years. As he was hanging up his coat, he collapsed and died. It was his first and last heart attack. He was seventy-two.

Will Rogers said: "We are all here for a spell, so get all the good laughs you can."

George did what the man said.

PART THREE

Hearsay

13

Pardon the Pun

"A pun is the lowest form of humour – when you don't think of it first."
Right on, Oscar Levant.

"Hanging is too good for a man who makes puns; he should be drawn and quoted."
A bull's-eye for you, Fred Allen.

For thousands of years, Man has had the urge to play around with words. In ancient Greece and Rome, such leading lights as Aristotle and Cicero were big promoters of the pun. It is said that King James the First of England was such an inveterate punster that he wouldn't appoint anyone a bishop or a privy counsellor unless the candidate could demonstrate that he was one too. Why, even Will Shakespeare was hooked; he peppered his writings with 1,062 puns.

"A pun is not bound by the laws which limit nicer wit," Charles Lamb wrote a couple of centuries ago. "It is a pistol let off at the ear; not a feather to tickle the intellect."

John S. Crosbie, punster extraordinaire and author of the delightful *Crosbie's Dictionary of Puns*, notes that "many people have in common an awkward reaction to hearing a pun. They try to reward the perpetrator by over-responding (usually with loud groans). This can be gratifying to the author's ego as long as the pun was intentional."

Devotees of the ancient and honourable art of punning will be pleased to learn that it still flourishes in the Canadian courts. Punsters inhabit the ranks of lawyers, judges and witnesses, and you never know when someone is going to deliver a "groaner."

Let's eavesdrop for a while.

Calgary lawyer Bruce J. Halliday reports a recent case in which several prisoners were charged with raping another inmate. The Crown Attorney suggested a particular trial date and the judge, with mock solicitude, asked defence counsel, "Will that date be satisfactory to your clients?"

Without a flicker of expression or a second's delay, the lawyer replied, "I suppose so, Your Honour. After all, buggers can't be choosers."

Mr. Justice William S. Tyndale of the Quebec Court of Appeal tells of a case heard in the Quebec Superior Court around 1960. A wife sued for annulment of her marriage, stating that her husband was hopelessly impotent. A doctor testified that the defendant had under-developed equipment, unsuitable for the use for which it was intended, and the trial judge, Associate Chief Justice George S. Challies, asked, "Wouldn't you expect such a man would realize his condition and refrain from marriage?"

"My Lord," the doctor replied, "we see this quite often in medical practice. It seems that such people suppose that if the occasion should arise they will rise to the occasion."

John B. Carrel, Q.C., of Thunder Bay, Ontario, sends this lulu.

In the 1940s there was a series of lawsuits between timber contractors in the Thunder Bay area. One of the central figures in the litigation was Walter Russell, who later became a well-respected magistrate in the district.

During one of the trials, Russell, a feisty character, was in the witness box for more than three days of continuous, gruelling cross-examination. The Supreme Court judge who presided was one of those "take charge" types who tend to take the trial away from counsel.

Russell, tired and irritated from his ordeal, had just testified that he was a graduate of the University of Michigan Law School and qualified to practise law in Michigan when His Lordship, who knew some of the faculty at the school, interrupted and asked if he knew Professor Bates.

"Yes," Russell snapped, "and I know his son, Master Bates!"

In Newfoundland, where a bottle of booze is often called a "jar," there was a judge who imbibed pretty heavily when he was on circuit. One morning, at Harbour Grace, the judge showed up in court with a black eye. He apologized for his appearance to the lawyers attending court, saying that on his way home the previous night he had bumped into a gate.

One of the lawyers asked, "Was the gate ajar, My Lord?"

The prosecutor was relating the facts to Provincial Court Judge Henry Murphy of Moncton, New Brunswick.

"Your Honour, the accused was found at the park with a bottle of liquor in his boot."

"Ha! Ha!" said the judge. "A bootlegger!"

Back in the thirties, a woman charged with vagrancy was brought before Magistrate K.M. Martin in Charlottetown, Prince Edward Island. She'd been found lounging in a railway freight car.

"Are you the one they call 'Box Car Annie?' " the magistrate asked after finding her guilty.

"That's me."

"Well, Annie, you're sidetracked for seven days."

The late Harold Riley, some of whose antics are reported elsewhere in these pages, was appointed *twice* to the Trial Division of the Supreme Court of Alberta. The story goes that very shortly after hearing the glad tidings for the first time, Mr. Riley departed for the Bahamas with a bevy of beauties. The Minister of Justice thought this a bit unseemly and so his appointment was revoked and another lawyer, Jimmy Cairns, was appointed in his stead.

As the judges were leaving the dais, at the conclusion of the swearing-in of Mr. Justice Cairns, a lawyer called out: "There goes Cairns, living the life of Riley!"

Mr. Justice James Mitchell Cairns himself was no slouch when it came to punning. In a bestiality case involving a man and a pig, he delivered a line that's considered to be a western classic.

Three neighbours testified against the accused farmer, but since all three denied reporting the incident and there were no other witnesses, defence counsel submitted that their evidence was not trustworthy.

"My Lord," the lawyer said, "if they were the only persons who allegedly saw anything, and they deny reporting anything to the authorities, who *did* report this alleged incident? How did the authorities even know about it?"

"Maybe the pig squealed," Mr. Justice Cairns suggested.

In a recent British Columbia damage action, the plaintiff had finished his testimony, during which he'd told several obvious fibs, and the trial judge asked the defendant's lawyer if he had any questions he wished to ask.

"No, thank you, My Lord," the lawyer replied. "I'm quite content to let lying dogs sleep."

Contempt of court proceedings were brought against a Saskatchewan trade union, and in the course of his testimony a union representative was explaining the inner workings of his organization.

"Are you saying that there was a certain pecking order in the union?" asked Mr. Justice D.C. Disbery.

"Yes, sir . . . sort of," the witness answered.

And His Lordship asked, "Are you a big pecker or a little pecker?"

In a rape case involving a man and a woman who both resided in the town of Bon Accord, Alberta, counsel for the defence told the Alberta Court of Appeal, "It couldn't have been rape; they were both of Bon Accord."

Ronald H. Brooks, a St. Catharines, Ontario, lawyer, recounts the case of a young man who pleaded guilty to a charge of stealing a package of condoms from a local drug store. The prosecutor – Mr. Brooks himself – told the judge the case didn't appear to be premeditated but rather was done "on the sperm of the moment."

In another case in St. Catharines, a package of toilet paper had been stolen from a store but a charge of theft was withdrawn because there wasn't enough evidence to implicate the accused. His lawyer said the charge was "a bum wrap." (Sodomy, by the way, has also been described as a "bum rap" and I heard of a case where the evidence of sodomy was so weak that the defence lawyer offered to plead his client guilty to a charge of "following too closely.")

Ottawa lawyer Colin McKinnon, Q.C., fondly recalls a case he prosecuted about ten years ago. Two "hippies" had spent the night fornicating on the lawn of the National Arts Centre. Several citizens took in the show. The pair were interrupted in mid-act by a policeman, who waltzed them off to jail. Later they pleaded guilty to a charge of performing sexual intercourse in a public place.

Senior Provincial Court Judge Glenn Strike, a veteran of forty years on the Bench, said he'd never before encountered a case of that nature, so he had no precedent to guide him.

McKinnon suggested to the court that the couple might join the cast of the musical, *Oh Calcutta!* "Perhaps that's why they were there," he suggested, tongue in cheek, "as a protest against the Arts Centre's refusal to stage the show."

Judge Strike struck a blow for morality, lecturing them on their behaviour and announcing that he was fining them twenty-five dollars or two days in jail.

Deadpan, he said, "That's twenty-five dollars *a piece.*"

Patrick Ryan, Q.C., of Fredericton, New Brunswick, tells of a similar situation which occurred in the early 1960s. One Saturday night, on the main street of Fredericton, a young couple made passionate love in the back seat of a car. A group of passersby, some amused and some shocked, peered through the car windows, which were becoming increasingly fogged up.

Someone summoned the cop on the beat, who thumped his night stick on the car roof and hollered for the couple to cease and desist.

No case of coitus interruptus, this. The lovers ignored the officer until they had attained rapturous release, whereupon they were arrested and charged with obstructing a peace officer in the execution of his duty. They pleaded guilty before Provincial Court Judge Lloyd B. Smith and were fined.

Visiting in court that day was another Provincial Court judge, colourful Charlie Tweeddale, who was somewhat of a legend in his jurisdiction of Oromocto and Minto, N.B.

When the case was over, Tweeddale told Judge Smith that the policeman should have been charged with "disturbing the piece," then added, "Lloyd, you should have found that young fellow not guilty. He was charged with the wrong offence. He should have been charged under the Shipping Act – for 'unlawful discharge of se(a)men.' "

Neil D. MacLean, Q.C., an outstanding counsel in Edmonton for over half a century, often crossed swords with the firm of Shortreed, Shortreed and Stanton, who prosecuted cases on behalf of the Crown. The firm consisted of William Shortreed, his son Jack and a very sombre man named William Stanton.

One morning, all three of them were conferring at the foot of the steps outside of the Edmonton Court House when "Neil D.," frisky following a victory over one of the trio, skipped lightly down the steps, tipped his homburg and exclaimed: "Well, well, well, the Father, the Son and the Holy Ghost!"

Garry K.C. Braund, Q.C., of Toronto, showed up in Provincial Court one day wearing a multi-coloured sports jacket.

"That's quite a coat you're wearing," noted the judge. "Is the circus in town?"

"Yes, Your Honour," Braund replied, "and I'm in charge of carnival knowledge."

On another occasion, a client of Braund's was charged with break and enter. The Crown brought a broken window into court, the same window which the accused had allegedly broken to gain entry. It rested on the counsel table, awaiting the testimony of a fingerprint expert who, presumably, would state that the accused's prints were all over it.

When the time came to present the window in evidence, the Crown Attorney picked it up – and dropped it. It broke into smithereens.

"Your Honour," Braund said, "I submit the Crown's case has gone to pieces."

Gordon Kuski, Q.C., of Regina, appeared in a case in which four men were charged with conspiracy to defraud the Minister of National Revenue. The trial took six weeks and, towards the end, some of the lawyers were becoming quite testy.

The Crown, which had already called five expert witnesses, sought leave to call a sixth. One of the defence lawyers, Greg Brodsky of Winnipeg, objected strenuously, stating that the Criminal Code permitted the Crown to call five experts, but no more.

"I can count on one hand the number of witnesses they're entitled to call," Brodsky said, "and that should be the limit."

Kuski said he agreed with what Brodsky had said, but he had another reason to object to the calling of a sixth expert – he would be giving "second-hand evidence."

In the early 1960s, the British Columbia government expropriated the shares of B.C. Electric Company. The result was a big lawsuit in which a great many people sought fair compensation for lost shares.

The defence called a renowned expert on the valuation of shares, a man from Philadelphia whose last name was Friend. He talked down to everyone.

When he couldn't take any more of Friend's condescension, Vancouver lawyer Douglas Brown exclaimed: "The Salvation Army Band should be here playing 'Oh, What a Jesus We Have in Friend!' "

A few years back, Her Honour Janet Boland, Judge of the County Court of the County of York, was promoted to the Supreme Court of Ontario. This would make her Madam Justice Boland.

Crown Attorney Ted Kielb, of Toronto, along with others, was asked to speak at the swearing-in ceremony. This was his salute:

"It's nice to see a lady like you giving up 'Your Honour' to be a 'Madam.' "

It was a divorce trial and the issue was whether the defendant and co-respondent had committed adultery.

The defendant testified that he and the co-respondent drove to a secluded spot, took the seat from the front of the car and put it a few feet away, but all they did, he insisted, was sit on the seat and listen to music on the car radio.

Mr. Justice Walter Schroeder, of the Ontario Supreme Court, was highly skeptical. "You only listened to music?" he asked the man, withering him with a glare.

"Yes, My Lord."

"Was it mountain music?"

Serge Kujawa, Q.C., of Regina, was arguing a case for the Crown in the Saskatchewan Court of Appeal. The case had to do with Native land and whether the Natives were entitled to be compensated for damage thereto. Kujawa upheld the negative.

One of the panel of judges said to Kujawa, "You say the Indians should receive no compensation?"

The lawyer replied: "Not a Sioux, My Lord."

Calgary lawyer Jack Major, Q.C., was one of the defence counsel in an interesting criminal case heard a few years back. A suspected drug pusher was arrested at the Edmonton airport. Suspecting that he was carrying drugs, the police took him to a hospital, where doctors conducted a thorough search of his rectal canal and environs. The man sued for damages, alleging he'd been assaulted.

Jack Major argued that the court shouldn't bother to hear the case but should order that it be decided by the Right of Entry Arbitration Board.

About fifteen years ago, Toronto criminal lawyer Bill Murphy represented a man who was charged with being a "found-in" after police raided a bawdy house. Proud of his unblemished record, the man fought the charge, but he had a very weak case – mainly because he was caught in the act. When police barged in, they saw the accused and a prostitute named Rita Paradis doing what comes naturally.

The proper pronunciation of the woman's last name was "Paradee," but the morality detectives who testified pronounced it as if it were "Paradise." "Miss Paradise" did this, "Miss Paradise" did that.

Murphy knew the jig was up. The police had his man cold. He told the judge his client was a harmless man, a forlorn fellow who was alone in the big city. The accused, he said, was just "a stranger in Paradise."

Ralph S. Mills, Q.C., of Toronto, recalls the time his friend George Walsh, Q.C., cracked off a good one in a bitterly contested divorce and custody case in Welland, Ontario. Most of the time during the three-day trial was taken up with out-of-court discussions on custody. The issues were finally settled, counsel went back into court and Walsh announced the detailed custody terms that had been agreed to.

"And now, My Lord," he told Mr. Justice P.E. Smily, "as we have reached the correct collusion I assume you will grant the divorce as a matter of course."

Morris Shumiatcher, Q.C., of Regina, was in fine fettle during a drinking-driving case. The prosecutor was an attractive, buxom young lady who kept asking her witnesses "leading" questions. Shumiatcher objected every time she committed this no-no, and every one of his objections was upheld by the trial judge.

When Shumiatcher cross-examined the Crown witnesses he asked leading questions too. The Crown Attorney objected every time he did it and the judge overruled all her objections.

"I don't know why my friend persists in doing this," Shumiatcher told the judge. "She should know that it's perfectly proper to ask leading questions on *cross*-examination."

"That may be so," the prosecutor said, "but this is a case of tit for tat."

Shumiatcher shot back: "That's what's wrong, Your Honour. My gentle tats are no match for my friend's tits!"

Ottawa lawyer John ("Jake") Dunlap represented a man whose car soared off the road one night and smashed into a post. The investigating officer and two other witnesses testified that the vehicle struck with such force that they could read the number of the licence plate on the post.

The prosecutor, a painfully thorough fellow, grilled all three witnesses about the damage to the post and asked them umpteen other questions, such as: "Exactly what time did this happen on Saturday evening?" and "What was the weather like that Saturday evening?" and "What were the driving conditions like that Saturday evening?" and "Was there much traffic at that location that Saturday evening?"

Jake, exasperated, finally interjected and suggested: "Your Honour, perhaps we should refer to this as The Saturday Evening Post."

Kenneth Houston, Q.C., of Winnipeg, speaks with awe and admiration of William Parker Fillmore, Q.C., as does every lawyer who ever saw the man in action. Fillmore was an outstanding counsel who practised in Winnipeg for about sixty years. Since the early days of this century, stories of his sparkling wit have been told countless times throughout Western Canada and beyond.

About twenty-five years ago, when Ken Houston was a rookie lawyer, the legendary Fillmore scared him half to death, yet left him laughing heartily.

Houston launched an action on behalf of a client who shipped a large cargo of live frogs from Winnipeg to the U.S. for research purposes. The frogs were in jute bags and the driver of the transport truck which carried them was supposed to water down the bags every now and then.

The driver took his girlfriend with him, contrary to company rules, and, being otherwise occupied, he gave none of his attention to the frogs. When he arrived at his destination, he discovered to his horror that most of the frogs were dead. Shortly thereafter, he and his employer were sued for a hefty amount.

"Before my young friend speaks," the formidable Mr. Fillmore said at the outset of a pre-trial motion brought by Houston, "I have a motion of my own which I'd like to bring. I move that the entire statement of claim be struck out."

"Holy shit! What have I done wrong?" Houston recalls asking himself in terror. He knew that if Fillmore's motion succeeded, the lawsuit was as dead as the frogs. As Fillmore continued to speak, Houston continued to gulp – hard.

"Paragraph seven of my friend's statement of claim states that 'in the course of the said carriage many of the said frogs died,' " Mr. Fillmore began gravely. "Your Lordship, that's totally wrong, totally wrong."

"What do you submit it should say?" the judge inquired.

"It should say 'many of the said frogs croaked!' "

W.P. Fillmore loved making puns. To him, the pun was the highest form of humour, and he grabbed every opportunity he could to unload one.

Many of his puns had an elaborate background, such as this one, which is a favourite of master raconteur Samuel Freedman, former Chief Justice of Manitoba:

Addressing first-year students at the University of Manitoba Law School, Fillmore noted the presence of Harvey Straight, longtime lecturer and registrar at the school. He said that seeing Mr. Straight in his audience reminded him of an American murder case in which the accused's last name was Straight.

The case attracted a great deal of public attention, Fillmore said, and one day a housewife, listening to the radio in her kitchen, heard a bulletin announcing the jury's decision. She went upstairs to tell the news to her husband, who was in the bathroom.

"She opened the door just as her husband was stepping into the bathtub," Fillmore said, "and told him: 'They're not hanging Straight.'"

You may groan if you wish. And, while you're at it, you might want to bestow the same sort of accolade upon Ken Matthews, Q.C., of Truro, Nova Scotia, for this offering:

Matthews defended a black man, some twenty-five years ago, whose first name was Paris. He was charged with hijacking a truckload of liquor. In investigating the heist, the R.C.M.P. came up with a witness who said he'd seen the accused at the scene, with the aid of the headlights of his car. Matthews doubted this, since it was a very dark night and his client was black. The client insisted he'd had absolutely nothing to do with the crime.

"Do you have any brothers, Paris?" Matthews asked. He did, and one of them looked very much like him.

Matthews arranged to interview the Crown witness and he picked him up in his car the night before the trial. The interview took place in the car, which was parked under a strong street light. There were three people in the vehicle – Matthews and the Crown witness in the front and a black man, sitting quietly, unintroduced, in the back.

The next day, at trial, the prosecutor called the star witness, who positively identified the accused as the person he had seen taking the liquor from the truck.

In cross-examination, Matthews had the witness recount the events of the previous night. The more he was cross-examined the more the witness was certain that the man seated in the back of the car the evening before was the accused, the same person he'd seen pulling the robbery. He was absolutely certain of this, even though on the night of the crime he'd had only a fleeting glimpse of the criminal in the headlights of his vehicle. He said that last night he'd had a much better look at him, since they were in the same car together.

It looked like the jig was up for Paris until his lawyer turned around, pointed to the rear of the courtroom and said dramatically, "Stand up, please!"

Paris' brother rose to his feet.

"*This* was the man you saw in the car last night!" Matthews said to the witness. "Can you deny it?"

"No, I can't."

The witness then admitted that he couldn't positively identify the accused as the person he saw on the night of the robbery. It was "game over" for the Crown.

Heady with success, and wanting one more shot at the witness, Matthews said: "Tell me, when was the last time you saw Paris?"

In Toronto, a man charged with possession of drugs for the purpose of trafficking asked to be released on bail. It was alleged that he had swallowed several condoms full of hashish oil and, naturally, the authorities didn't want him to get away on them until they'd had a chance to recover the evidence.

The Crown Attorney and defence lawyer agreed that the accused should be released on bail, but not until he'd had three bona fide bowel movements.

It was explained to the court that each of these momentous events would be closely monitored. All movements were to be deposited into a chamber pot under the scrutiny of a member of the Royal Canadian Mounted Police, and it was the duty of this lucky fellow to check each movement "minutely." He could hardly wait to plunge into action.

The judge asked defence counsel if his client agreed to this arrangement. The lawyer said his client had no objection. Then the judge asked the lawyer, "Do you have any idea what you're doing to that Mountie?"

"What do you mean, Your Honour?"

"Why, you're turning him into a stool pigeon!"

Percy Hagel was a fascinating rascal who practised law for many years in Winnipeg. In 1914, he helped to smuggle a rope and a pistol to a client being held on a murder charge, thus enabling him to make a spectacular break from prison. The man was later recaptured, convicted and hanged, and for his shameful part in things Hagel was jailed and disbarred.

After his release from prison, Percy became an itinerant evangelist for a while. He could have given hypocrisy lessons to Elmer Gantry. Roaming the countryside, preaching the glories of God and the evils of intemperance, he often demonstrated the latter by his own boozy behaviour between services.

Hagle must have been a persuasive advocate because a few years after his release from jail he talked the Manitoba Law Society into letting him resume practice. The Law Society often regretted its charitable decision; Percy was in and out of trouble for the rest of his life.

"It can't be denied, however, that his career greatly enriched the mythology of the Manitoba legal profession," Professor Dale Gibson, of the University of Manitoba Faculty of Law, has written.

Even the manner of his death, in 1944, is the subject of stories. One story in particular:

It is said that when Percy Hagel died he was locked in the embrace of a scarlet woman, who later told a reporter, sadly, "When he trembled, I thought he was coming. But I guess he was going."

14

Oops!

Move over, Dick Clark and Ed McMahon. Enough of your TV bloopers. Give the lawyers, judges, witnesses and secretaries a chance to show their stuff.

Typographical errors and slips of the tongue crop up regularly in the Canadian legal world. They often trigger a grin or a chuckle or a guffaw. Sometimes they make your day. I say, fervently, God bless the unwitting perpetrators thereof.

First, some typos.

A Calgary court reporter, Lawrence Lebitka, found this delightful miscue in the transcribed evidence of a witness in a break-and-enter case:

"I saw a form half in and half out of the widow."

Court reporter Jim Flannery, also of Calgary, wondered what was going on when he spotted this one in a transcript. At the conclusion of a Land Compensation Board hearing, the Chairman told the lawyers:

"Well, gentlemen, unless there is anything else, I think that concludes this case. I would like to express my own and the Board's appreciation to counsel for their clear and defective presentation."

A lawyer named Whittaker probably wasn't amused (but others were) to see himself described in a transcript as "Mr. Shittaker." And that reminds me – Edmonton court reporter Barb MacGillivray turned in this example of a teeney-weeney typo: "The Court (in dismissing a jury): So if you wish to go, you may do do."

And since we're on the subject, consider this Alberta specimen:

Q. Have you required any other medical aids aside from the cast and the back brace and the canes? Is there anything else that you used?
A. Just pillows when I sleep of shit.

I'm indebted to a Manitoba court reporter, Yvonne Kemp, for this amusin' but confusin' goof:

Q. You have admitted, have you not, to engaging in an adulterous relationship with this young lady during the time that you were still legally married to my client?
A. Yes, sir.
Q. What I want to know is this: At what point in time did this adulterous relationship commence between you and your power mower?

Ray Cuthbert, Chief Supreme Court Reporter for Ontario, points out that, "Reporters dictate a great many of their notes on cases to freelance typists who are not always on the same wavelength, and errors creep in which make proofreading essential."

He gives an example from an inquiry into the sinking of a ship:

Q. Sir, you say you were on the bridge just prior to the emergency situation. Where were you when the shit hit the fan?

This was corrected by the reporter to "ship hit the sand."
And from the same inquiry:

Q. Madam, I take it as a biologist you have been dealing a great deal with plankton, seaweed of various sorts and orgasms at sea?

In fairness to humans, it should be noted that not all typographical errors can be pinned on typists. Some are caused by computers. Since the advent of "Computer Aided Transcription" a few years ago, "CAT bloopers" have become common. Here's one:

Q. Sir, you received Sex B benefits as a result of this accident?

Here's another:

COUNSEL: Your Honour, that concludes my matters for today. May I expose myself?
These computers seem to have dirty minds.

Hey, I thought we'd abolished capital punishment in this country. Obviously, the computer hasn't heard the news:
CROWN: Your Honour, I would ask for a warrant for Mr. Smith and I ask that he be executed.

But we mustn't blame everything on poor, defenceless machines. Human beings still cause most of the verbal carnage. Screwed-up syntax plays havoc. Even learned editors of law reports fall victim to it.

For example, in the 1957 edition of *Ontario Weekly Notes*, a law-report service, the opening sentence in a report of the case of *Regina* v. *Fargnoli* reads as follows: "An appeal from conviction by a County Court Judge of indecently assaulting his daughter." (No wonder the judge convicted Fargnoli. I'd convict anyone who messed around with *my* daughter.)

In the Supreme Court of Canada Reports of 1971, in the case of *Loos* v. *The Queen*, it is stated that: "The appellant was convicted of indecent assault by a magistrate without a jury." What one missing comma can do! I can't help wondering: Would it have been a more serious offence if the assault had been committed by a magistrate *with* a jury?

Secretaries, God bless 'em, slip up occasionally.

Marie Lalonde, who is a secretary to a Federal Court judge, confessed to me a "terrible error" she'd made when she was a junior secretary in a law office. She typed a letter to an elderly client, enclosing a copy of his newly typed will, and addressed him as "Dead Sir." Here's the sequel, in Marie's own words:

"At the time I was truly embarrassed but our client found it most funny and said he was glad he was 'alive' to see he was 'dead.' After the initial embarrassment wore off, I too saw the funny side of it, thanks mainly to our client's super sense of humour."

To err is human, to forgive divine.

Ms. Lalonde will appreciate this anecdote, sent by Adam Germain, a lawyer in Fort McMurray, Alberta:

"A junior secretary working in our firm a few years ago was typing a letter, one sentence of which read: 'We regret to inform you that our client died intestate' [i.e., without a will]. After finishing that sentence she looked up and asked the other secretaries: 'Does anyone know where Testate, Alberta is?' "

In a brief submitted to the Supreme Court of Canada, a sentence started with the words: "In the Court of Appeal, the Appellant drove to Barrie . . . " One of the judges wondered what that was all about. Had the Appellant decided to get away from it all, or what? The embarrassed lawyer, who obviously hadn't proofread the brief nor studied it closely when preparing for the appeal, said sheepishly that the sentence should have read: "In the Court of Appeal, the Appellant strove to vary . . . "

Mr. Justice Allan Wachowich, of the Alberta Court of Queen's Bench, was flipping through the court documents during a divorce trial when he noticed this statement:

"The panties have been separated on numerous occasions."

At the end of the case, the petitioner's lawyer said he had no further evidence to present. Mr. Justice Wachowich asked him if he was going to call some evidence on the panties. The lawyer looked at the petition and said, "Oh, Jesus, no!"

Sad but true, typos are epidemic.

"Res ipsa loquitur" is a Latin phrase familiar to all lawyers. It means "the thing speaks for itself."

A lawyer dictated a sentence that ended with the words "and the plaintiff says 'res ipsa loquitur.' " It came out as follows: "and the plaintiff says 'raise the hips and lock the door.' "

Another Alberta divorce petition was also in sad shape. The phrase "just and equitable" appears in many court documents, and it was supposed to show up a few times in this one, too. Here are some of the matters the wife asked the court to grant:

> "(d) Interim and permanent maintenance for the infant children in an amount that is just inequitable;
>
> (e) Interim and permanent maintenance for the plaintiff in an amount that is just inequitable;
>
> (f) Lump sum payment in an amount that is just inequitable;
>
> (g) Such further and other relief as to this Honourable Court may seem just inequitable."

Professor Dale Gibson, of the Faculty of Law of the University of Manitoba, dictated a document concerning bankruptcy and creditors. A secretary mangled one of the sentences and it ended up looking like this:
"This priority applied only as against unsecured predators."

In 1983, an Edmonton policeman gave a speeding ticket to a Virginia man. The officer wrote on the ticket that the speeder lived at a certain address in "Arlington, Vagina." He was going off duty at the time.

Poor syntax can also knock a spoken sentence out of kilter, as it did with the judge who started his address to a jury with these words:
"Now, as we begin, I must ask you to banish all present information and prejudice from your minds, if you have any."

It also helps to have the right words lined up, ready for action. A Citizenship judge, addressing a batch of new Canadians, thrust his foot far into his mouth by declaring, "One of the best ways of learning about native-born Canadians is to have intercourse with them – er, I mean discourse with them."
Shucks, some of them probably thought the first idea was better.

People get used to talking in a certain way and it's often hard for them to teach their mouths new tricks. Take, for example, the western witness who said "M-hmmm" instead of "Yes." He used the expression over and over again, and the judge tried to put him straight on this simple but important matter.

THE COURT: Will you answer 'yes' or 'no,' please, because when it is recorded it is very difficult for the girl taking notes to know if you mean 'yes' or 'no.' All right?

A. M-hmmm.

Judicial tongues can also slip out of gear, especially when the judge is new in the saddle. The sudden transition from advocate to judge requires an adjustment in point of view that isn't easy to get the hang of overnight. For the first while, they say, the judge is still thinking like a lawyer.

Before he was a judge, Mr. Justice P.J. Montague practised for many years in the civil courts of Manitoba. Shortly after he went on the Bench, he found himself hearing an automobile accident case in which a former partner of his appeared for one of the parties. Concentrating intently on his former partner's introductory remarks on the facts he hoped to prove, His Lordship must have thought momentarily that he was back in his old office, for he asked, "And which was our fellow's car?"

Freudian slips have it over any other kind, I verily believe. They're the most revealing, and they're usually the most humorous.

In a wedding ceremony performed in a Winnipeg courtroom, the bride promised resignedly to take her rather seedy-looking groom as her "awful wedded husband." Louise Johnston, a North Vancouver lawyer, tells about friends of hers who were married by a judge. They were both middle-aged and avid sailors, and when they tied the knot the groom promised to take the lady as his "awful weathered wife."

A Vancouver lawyer obviously didn't think much of his opponent's case. He told the court his learned friend was "caught on the horns of an enema."

In January, 1985, an eighteen-year-old prostitute, in custody on a robbery charge in Edmonton, appeared before Mr. Justice Edward P. MacCallum of the Court of Queen's Bench of Alberta and asked to be released on bail. The Crown Attorney leaped to his feet and objected strenuously, voicing his fear that the woman would commit further robberies while at large.

"She is, after all, My Lord, a drug addict," the prosecutor stated. Then, pointing to the inside of his arms, he said: "The police tell me she has pecker tra – Oh, my God, I meant to say needle tracks, on both arms."

His Lordship reports: "There followed profuse apologies from the unfortunate fellow, whose discomfiture was not alleviated by the merriment of everyone else in court – including me."

A few years back, a Manitoba Supreme Court judge heard a rape case in which the accused claimed that the woman in question had consented and she said that she had only agreed to have coffee with him.
    In addressing the jury, the judge made a honey of a Freudian slip:
    "Now, ladies and gentlemen, the complainant says she went with the accused for the sole purpose of having a piece of coffee."

Another lulu occurred several years ago in Vancouver, and court reporter Barbara Purvis had the presence of mind to record it.
    After a lengthy and rather tedious trial, and before handing down his decision, the judge turned to the accused and asked, "Is there anything you wish to say on your own behalf, Mr. Guilty?"

15

Stupid Questions

Let's hear it for Doreen Johnson. She likes to make you laugh.

Doreen isn't a comedienne, but she can tickle your funny bone.

She's an Edmonton court reporter with an interesting, fun-filled hobby. She works tirelessly in her spare time to "capture" courtroom quips and bloopers that lie buried in transcripts of evidence, thus preserving them for posterity. In a way she's a historian.

Ms. Johnson collects these verbal gems – she calls them "trans-quips" – the way others collect butterflies, and presents them periodically in a newsmagazine she edits for the Alberta Shorthand Reporters Association. It's a treasure-trove of humour – mostly unintentional – from the Alberta courts. In my view, this jolly little journal does more to promote mental health than a phalanx of psychiatrists could in a month of Sundays.

Doreen always has an eagle eye peeled for Stupid Questions. When she spots one, she pounces on it and impales it immediately so that her readers can enjoy it in the next issue of her magazine.

Our courts have borne witness to some incredibly stupid questions, asked by lawyers and judges who were either incredibly stupid themselves or had succumbed to battle fatigue. Whatever the reason, you can be sure that in each instance the perpetrator had switched off his brain for a time.

The following is one of Doreen's all-time favourites. The veteran court reporter who donated it to a grateful public says it's the highlight of his long career:

Q. Now isn't it true that when a person dies in his sleep, in most cases he just passes quietly away and doesn't know anything about it until the next morning? (When, presumably, he reads about it in the paper.)

That's definitely a major-league Stupid Question and in my view it should be considered the standard against which all others are measured. Any interrogator who can match or surpass that doozie should be waived straight into the Hall of Shame, with no waiting period. But there are some truly great contenders, such as this one:

"The twenty-fourth of December – was that the day before Christmas?"

And you have to give a big hand to this hot prospect:
Q. Were you acquainted with the deceased?
A. Yes.
Q. Before or after he died?

Only someone like MacKenzie King could have thought of a question like that.

Let's take a closer look at the Doreen Johnson Collection. What follows (unless otherwise indicated) is an anthology of asinine questions she compiled from transcripts that have crossed her desk. These lulus all come from the courts of Alberta, but this doesn't mean that Albertans are more stupid than others, let me assure you. It's just that Alberta appears to be the only province where this sort of research has been done. When it is done elsewhere, I hope someone will send me the details in a plain brown wrapper.

Q. The land in Portugal; is it still there?

Q. How many children – she had three? Right?
A. Yes.
Q. How many were boys?
A. None.
Q. Were there girls?
A. Three girls.

Q. You remember that no one was touching her.
A. That's right.
Q. Who is that no one that wasn't touching her?
A. I don't know.

Q. Who were these trucks that you had discussions with?

Q. And how did you know the policeman wasn't a dog?

Secretaries will love this one:

A. You remember the person who was there. Was there a person or was it simply some sort of secretary that you were signing these in front of?

This lawyer has a very short memory:

Q. When I am asking you questions, I expect from you what you know yourself personally. All right? I don't want you giving us what somebody else might have told you or, like you say "I have an idea." Don't give us these ideas unless you know personally. Okay?

A. Okay.

Q. All right. Can you give me an idea . . . ?

In another case reported by Ms. Johnson, we're treated to a whole bunch of Stupid Questions from a lawyer who examined a farmer who was distressed in more ways than one:

Q. What has the property been used for over the past three years?

A. The previous two years, farming, and this year, nothing. They were droughted out so we never realized anything. The payments were being made out of the farm until the drought hit us.

Q. When is this drought you are talking about?

A. 1982.

Q. The spring of 1982?

A. Spring, summer and fall. Peace River country was 90 percent wiped out because of lack of rain.

Q. When did you last work?

A. Last fall when I put the crop in.

Q. How could you put the crop in if there was a flood?

A. Do I have to answer that?

Q. Yes.

A. I don't think it deserves answering.

Q. Why?

A. Because we didn't have a flood. I told you we had a drought.

Q. Drought. Sorry.

A. That's right, and you put your crops in in the spring. Do I have to explain the farming procedures to you?

Q. I'm sorry. You mentioned to me that you put in a crop last fall.

A. You don't put a crop in in the fall. You put it in in the spring and it grows in the summer.

Q. Do you own any farm equipment?
A. I have my name on a tractor.
Q. What kind of tractor?
A. A White tractor – and a Case 1030.
Q. That is a Case 1030 white tractor?
A. Yes.
Q. How much is owed on that?
A. $21,000 on the two of them.
Q. Two of what?
A. The two tractors.
Q. I only heard you describe one tractor.
A. I said I own two tractors, a White tractor and a Case. White is the name of the tractor.
Q. I'm sorry. I don't know much about tractors.

Through her newsmagazine, Doreen Johnson encourages other Alberta court reporters to rescue court humour from oblivion. Some of her colleagues have come up with sparkling gems, such as this one, snared by Christie Stone in Provincial Court in Edmonton:

Q. "And you are how old a woman, sir?"

Karen Swartzenberger preserved this dandy:

A. And then I read the demand to the accused.
Q. Did you read it from a card or from the top of your head?
(That cop must be a contortionist.)

Thanks to another Alberta court reporter, Rosemary Aitken, we can admire the handiwork of this scintillating cross-examiner:

Q. Who else was with you in your van?
A. There was no one else.
Q. Were you alone, then?
A. Yeah.
Q. And you were the driver? Is that right?
A. Yeah.

Colin Spencer, a lawyer in Rosetown, Saskatchewan, says that the dumbest question he's heard in court came from a senior counsel who asked an eyewitness to a car accident, "In your opinion, how far apart were the vehicles at the time of the collision?"

In a complicated criminal case in Ontario, a top counsel, punchy from a welter of technical evidence about soundwaves and decibels, switched off his brain for a moment and asked an expert this Stupid Question:

"Witness, give me an example of some sounds that you have heard that are outside the range of human hearing."

Michael Hutchison, a lawyer in Victoria, British Columbia, read in my legal humour column that I thought some lawyers should be rushed into the Hall of Shame because of the stupidity of their questions. He nominates his opponent in a recent immigration case, a case, he hastens to add, which he won for the defence.

"You cannot ask that witness to tell you what he was told by someone else," the judge scolded the prosecutor. "If you want that evidence you will have to get it some other way."

"Very well, then. Witness, without telling me what he said to you, what did he tell you to say?"

Recently I received a truly great Stupid Question from Vancouver court reporter Barbara Purvis. This memorable utterance from Provincial Court in Vancouver a few years ago may well be unparalleled in Canadian forensic history. Let's hear all about it from Barbara herself:

"During the trial of an alleged purse-snatcher, Crown Counsel was trying to prove that when the accused pushed his victim to the sidewalk, she sustained very bad bruises and cuts to her knees. In fact, bad enough that the evidence was still visible.

"Crown Counsel wanted his witness to show her scars to the judge. The victim, a little, elderly lady, was very shy and reluctant to lift her skirts for the judge's scrutiny. Finally, after much gentle persuasion by Crown Counsel, she consented.

"All was quiet in the courtroom, with every eye scanning the knees of the unfortunate lady. At last the tension was broken when Crown Counsel intoned:

" 'And are those the same knees that you were wearing on the day in question?' "

When I wrote about that humdinger in my column, the most amazing thing happened. The perpetrator turned himself in. He's Robert G. DeBou, a Vancouver lawyer and a great sport, if ever there was one. He wrote, "I felt compelled to express my appreciation to you for bestowing on me the nomination for Hall of Shame recognition which I feel that classic question so richly deserves."

Don't mention it, Bob. You really deserve the honour. But you have another one for me? One of your own?

"Only months after that incident, I formulated another brilliant question for a police officer who attended a break-in of business premises, to wit: 'Officer, was the silent alarm still ringing when you arrived at the scene?' "

That's not as good as the knees one, Bob, but it's not bad. I know you plan to keep trying because your letter ends on an upbeat note by saying:

"I still have aspirations of one day surpassing that career milestone which you have so kindly immortalized."

Bob also told me about the Vancouver lawyer, another ex-Crown attorney, who asked, "What colour were the blue jeans?"

Then, as if he hasn't helped me enough already, he blows the whistle on another lawyer, so far unidentified, who asked these immortal questions:

Q. "How long have you known your brother?"
Q. "Were you alone or by yourself?"
Q. "How long have you been a French Canadian?"

So much talent in *one* guy! It's awesome.

16

Words

"A very great part of the mischiefs that vex this world arises from words."
Edmund Burke certainly knew what he was talking about.

Take court, for example. Quite a few centuries ago, Man abandoned the charming practice of settling disputes by mortal combat and switched to verbal combat. From then on, differences were to be resolved through a process of testimony, argument and reasoning. Why, a person could lose a case and still live to talk about it! Yes, swords, spears, clubs and fists were out; words were in.

Words became, and still are, the raw material of the courts. Trials without words are as inconceivable as baseball without a ball or hockey without a puck. And the words that are used in the legal world are often bashed around as much as any ball or puck. Words get scuffed up through misuse and misunderstanding, often with hilarious results. Let's examine some of the evidence.

Maria Mihailovich, of Hamilton, Ontario, editor of a newsletter called the *Chartered Shorthand Reporter*, sends this exhibit:

Q. I take it that before this accident happened you lived with your brother-in-law and sister for about six months?
A. Yes.
Q. You got to know him quite well?
A. Yes.
Q. And you saw him interact with your sister, and I believe they had one child?
A. I didn't see the actual interaction, but they did have one child.

Ray Cuthbert, Chief Supreme Court Reporter for Ontario, reports the following dialogue from a case heard in Windsor:

Q. Mrs. Smith, you have already admitted in your evidence that you had sex with the co-respondent in London and on at least two occasions in Ottawa. Did you have any relations in Toronto?

A. No, but I have a brother and sister living in Sarnia.

Some people know a fair bit about adultery, right down to how to commit it, but they can't remember what the hell it's called.

A witness in an Alberta divorce case testified that he saw the respondent and co-respondent in a compromising position in the back of his car.

"What were they doing?" asked the trial judge, the late Mr. Justice Boyd McBride.

The embarrassed witness hemmed and hawed.

"You can tell us," the judge said. "What were they doing?"

"Well . . ."

"Yes?"

"They were committing perjury."

Oh, well, they *were* lying. Meanwhile, an Edmonton lawyer told me that a client had admitted to him that he'd had "intersection" with a certain woman. (On a corner, no doubt.)

Julien Payne, Q.C., a professor of law at the University of Ottawa, tells of the trouble a Saskatoon lawyer had in cross-examining a woman about her alleged adultery:

"Did you commit adultery?" the lawyer asked.

The woman gave him a blank stare.

"Did you commit *adultery*?" he asked, helping her quite a bit.

She looked askance.

The lawyer asked the question again, with the same added emphasis. As he asked it, he joined the thumb and index finger of his left hand to form a circle, and with the index finger of his right hand he imitated a piston engine.

The woman, getting the drift, replied. "Oh, *yes!*"

Mr. Justice Andre Dechene, of the Court of Queen's Bench of Alberta, is also a member of the Supreme Court of the Northwest Territories. He tells the story of an Inuit woman who was called as a Crown witness in a case against her husband.

An Inuktitut-English interpreter discussed the charge with the woman and briefed her to some extent on the types of questions she might be asked. She forgot, however, to explain the meaning of the "swearing-in" that would take place at the start of her testimony.

When the woman took the stand, the court clerk asked her the usual formula question: "Do you swear to tell the truth, the whole truth and nothing but the truth, so help you God?"

There was a long silence. The witness seemed very embarrassed and reluctant to say anything.

The presiding judge, the late Mr. Justice William G. Morrow, asked her: "Madam, do you not understand that it is necessary that you be sworn in before giving evidence? Do you understand the nature of the oath? Do you *swear* to tell the truth?"

The witness gazed at the floor and the ceiling, then demonstrated her understanding of the words "to swear." Turning to her husband, she exclaimed, "Charlie, you Goddamn son of a bitch!"

Vocabulary is the stumbling block of many a witness. Often a witness will guess at the meaning of a word and, fingers crossed, plough straight ahead.

David Friend, Q.C., of Toronto, defended a man for socking a fellow who had tried to rape the man's daughter. The case was adjourned five times and when it was finally heard Friend presented the background evidence and tried to establish that the punch was delivered in self-defence.

The accused was honest, however, and he admitted on cross-examination that the blow had not been struck in self-defence. Friend suggested that the complainant be given an opportunity to do a gentlemanly act and withdraw the charge.

"Do you want to withdraw the charge?" the magistrate asked.

"No," said the complainant. Then he added: "What will happen if I don't?"

"If you don't withdraw the charge, I'll have to adjudicate this matter," the magistrate replied.

"Oh, no!" the complainant said, "Don't adjudicate the matter! I've been here five times already and I can't afford to come back again!"

"Either withdraw the complaint or I'll adjudicate the matter," the magistrate repeated.

"All right, all right, I'll withdraw the complaint!"

And he did.

Arthur Slaght, K.C., the top criminal lawyer in Toronto in the 1930s, kayoed the chief Crown witness with a few fast jabs in a driving offence case.

"Was the accused verbose?" Slaght asked the investigating officer.

"I don't understand your question," he said.

"Did he talk a lot?"

"No."

"Was he lachrymose?"

"Pardon me."

"Did he cry a lot?"

"No."

"Was the accused bellicose?"

"Huh?"

"Did he want to fight?"

"Uh, no."

"Was he comatose?"

"What does that mean?"

"Was he asleep?"

"No."

"Your Honour, I have no further questions. This man doesn't know *anything*!"

After the jurors had stopped laughing they acquitted the accused.

About five years ago, two Nova Scotia doctors were charged with performing an abortion. The key prosecution witness was a woman who had undergone the alleged abortion.

As the case progressed it became increasingly obvious to defence counsel that the woman had been extensively "coached" by the Crown.

On direct examination she used all the correct medical terms for parts of her anatomy, including what she described as her "vagina." On cross-examination, however, the woman admitted that when first interviewed by the R.C.M.P. she had called that region her "Regina."

"I've heard it called a lot of things before, but never the Queen!" quipped defence counsel Kenneth M. Matthews, Q.C., of Truro, N.S., who won the case.

Toronto lawyer Bill Murphy recalls a Halifax case in which a woman testified about a fight she'd been involved in.

Asked the judge:

And the woman replied:

In Quebec, witnesses may testify in either French or English. Mr. Justice Anthime Bergeron, of the Quebec Superior Court, tells of a case in which a doctor who was much more fluent in French than English decided, nevertheless, to testify in English.

In the course of his testimony, the doctor spoke about the plaintiff's bronchitis, which in French is "bronchite." He wasn't familiar with the term "bronchitis," so he tried to say "bronchite" in English. It came out as "brown shit."

Mr. Justice Bergeron also relates the story of a Francophone, determined to testify in English, who kept calling the judge "Your Lordshit." After the third or fourth time, the judge said to the witness, "From now on, just call me George."

Nuances of language sometimes pose problems for translators. In Toronto, a few years ago, police bugged the residence of a man suspected of committing a crime. The man, a Pakistani, was eventually charged and brought to trial, at which an interpreter translated the evidence, including the evidence the prosecution had on tape.

One of the activities of the accused while he was being surreptitiously recorded included sex, and while so occupied he made remarks which the police thought relevant to the case. The interpreter translated everything, including the big moment in bed, which he said culminated in the words: "I've arrived! I've arrived!"

Lawyers can mix metaphors with the best of them. Take Neil Fleishman, for example. In a murder case back in the 1950s, Fleishman exhorted a Vancouver jury to "take the bull by the tail and look it right in the eye."

Chief Justice Allan McEachern, of the Supreme Court of British Columbia, chuckles when he recalls a case he argued when he was at the bar. His opponent was George Cumming, Q.C., of Vancouver. Here's His Lordship's recollection:

"George Cumming likes to dress up his arguments with many amusing and colourful expressions. He had me all tied up and worn out one day because in quick succession, and within a matter of a very few minutes, he alleged that I was caught on the horns of a dilemma, I was using a steam roller, I had set up and then knocked down a man of straw, I had pulled myself up by my bootstraps, I was blowing hot and cold, and, worst of all, I was hoist with my own petard. I couldn't possibly continue the argument in that state."

Newfoundlanders use wonderfully expressive language. Judge Seamus O'Regan, of the Provincial Court of Newfoundland, sends this example from a case he prosecuted years ago:

"Prosecuting a criminal negligence trial involving a motor vehicle in a rural, strongly Catholic community, my main witness appeared to be getting 'hostile.' In giving evidence, he denied ever having given a statement to the police and informed the Court that he could not remember anything on the night in question because he was 'loaded drunk.'

"Given leave by the Court to cross-examine the witness, I concentrated on his degree of drunkenness. When I asked him to describe exactly what he meant by being 'loaded drunk,' he replied: " 'Your Honour, I was so drunk that I wouldn't have known the Blessed Virgin if she was front on to me!'"

There's nothing funny about the act of rape. There are, however, many humorous things said at rape trials, most of them unintentional.

The victim in an Ontario case, for example, testified, "He tried to have annual intercourse with me." Court reporter Gail McGilvray advises that later in the same trial the accused himself said, "It took me a long time to get erected."

Patrick V. Rudden, Q.C., of Cornwall, Ontario, recalls a rape case in his hometown. The Crown Attorney, the late R. Percy Milligan, Q.C., grilled the accused in a playful way:

Q. Did you feel her knee?
A. (reluctantly) Yes.
Q. Did you feel her thigh?
A. (reluctantly) Yes.
Q. (with indignation) Did you feel any area higher than that?
A. (reluctantly) Yes.
Q. (very indignantly) Did you not feel remorse?
A. (most reluctantly) Yes, I had my hand on that too.

Former Ontario Chief Justice G.A. Gale tells of a memorable trial at which he presided. The accused was alleged to have raped an extremely attractive but rather dumb woman at Cherry Beach in Toronto. For much of the trial, she had judge and jury in silent fits of laughter with her answers, which to her were quite reasonable.

Defence counsel cross-examined the woman about the place where the act was alleged to have taken place, behind some bushes on the deserted beach.

"And did you find solitude there?" he asked.

She paused, she looked at the judge, looked at the jury, then fluttered her eyelashes and replied, "No, he wasn't there."

Vancouver lawyer Tony Pantages was cross-examining the spare driver of a large semi-tractor-trailer which had been involved in an accident. The substitute driver, who lived in Chetwynd, British Columbia, said he was riding in the cab of the vehicle and saw the accident happen, but the lawyer had been advised by investigators that in fact he had been reposing in the sleeper at the time of impact.

Pantages couldn't resist the temptation to show off his knowledge of Greek mythology:

Q. You say you were in the cab? I suggest, sir, that at the time of the accident you were in the sleeper.
A. No, sir, I was in the cab.
Q. I suggest that you were in the sleeper and that, further, you were in the arms of Morpheus.
A. I don't even know him. Does he live in Chetwynd?

In a civil case, a woman brought down the house with this dialogue:

Q. Have you ever appeared as a witness in a suit before?
A. Yes.
Q. Please tell the jury what suit it was.
A. It was a blue suit, with white collar and cuffs and white buttons all the way down the back.

Judges and lawyers sometimes get their syntax out of whack. From a trial at St. Catharines, Ontario, we have this example:

Q. And, Doctor, as a result of your examination of the plaintiff in this case, was the young lady pregnant?
A. The young lady was pregnant, but not as a result of my examination.

And Mr. Justice Lloyd McKenzie, of the British Columbia Supreme Court, once drafted a judgement in a case in which a difficult lady was suing her architect for deficiencies in the construction of her residence. Fortunately, His Lordship had an eagle-eyed secretary, who spotted and repaired this sentence:

"After Herculean efforts, the defendant gave up trying to please the lady on the spiral staircase because he knew she would never be satisfied by his efforts."

This sentence from an affidavit filed in a divorce case in British Columbia ain't so hot either: "I am informed by the petitioner and verily believe that she was pregnant for several months before her baby was born."

Sometimes a witness knows what he wants to say, but when he opens his mouth the wrong words come tumbling out.

An Alberta physician had that ghastly experience:

Q. Doctor, what treatment did you give this man?
A. I cleaned the wound, sutured it, and put him to bed with a nurse.

Now that's what I call medical attention! I tried to get the name of the doctor, in case I'm ever sick in his part of the country, but they wouldn't tell me. I bet there's a line-up of men all the way to B.C.

Here's another instance of a doctor tripping over his tongue:

Q. Do you think that this is a permanent condition, Doctor?
A. Well, it's temporarily permanent.

Like the woman who said she was slightly pregnant, I suppose.

Some witnesses can accomplish the impossible, it appears. A western court was treated to this exchange:

Q. And you didn't make any exclamation or outcry at the time it was alleged to have happened, within the hearing of any person, did you?
A. I did the next day.
Q. What happened then?
A. I woke up unconscious in the hospital.

Here's a gem, courtesy of Edmonton court reporter Doreen Johnson:

Q. Do you drink?
A. Yes. Well, not at the moment. I've been sober now going on three years. But before that I used to drink fluently.

In a personal injury trial in Calgary, the plaintiff, a woman who'd had many medical problems, was testifying as to her numerous doctors.

The name of the next doctor came up and counsel asked her, "And what kind of a doctor was he?"

The woman thought for a moment, then replied. "Oh . . . not bad."

Judge Walder White, Assistant Chief Judge of the Provincial Court of Alberta, Family and Youth Divisions, chuckles when he recalls the time a rookie court clerk read a Juvenile Deliquents Act charge to a fourteen- or fifteen-year-old girl. The clerk stated that between the fourteenth and twenty-fourth days of a certain month, the girl had committed the offence of "sexual immortality."

It appears that's what a Kingston, Ontario, woman was shooting for. A snippet from the transcript of her husband's testimony in a criminal case reads as follows:

Q. When you entered the bedroom, what did you see?
A. I saw my wife in bed with her power mower.

Some people don't seem to listen to the other guy. An Alberta court reporter, Robin Grigat, submits this exhibit:

Q. And did you bear arms, Constable?
A. Yes, it was a short-sleeved shirt.
Q. I'm sorry. Were you carrying a weapon?
A. No, I was not. I had no side arms on, no, but I had bare arms.

An Edmonton lawyer told his new receptionist that he'd be out for a while as he was going to "an Exam in Aid," lawyer-lingo for a certain kind of examination of a judgement debtor.

After he'd left, a client phoned and asked for him.

"He won't be back till later this afternoon," the receptionist said. "He's being examined for Aids."

A statement of claim prepared by a British Columbia lawyer alleged that at the time of an accident the defendant was driving "erotically."

District Court Judge Sam Filer, of Brampton, Ontario, recalls a woman who consulted him when he was in practice. She asked him to prepare a "power of eternity" for her.

Norman Shepherd, Q.C., of Kincardine, Ontario, tells about a local lush who went into a pub, was served one drink and then was told to hit the road and never come back. He was furious about it – so furious that he was going to sue for "definition of character."

For years, Ontario lawyers debated as to who was the best criminal lawyer in the province: Arthur Martin or John Robinette. One day the late Arthur Maloney, a great lawyer himself, overheard two men talking in Toronto. One man said he'd been charged with a serious criminal offence and the other asked if he had a good lawyer.

"The best in Canada!" the accused boasted. "A man called Martinette."

A few years ago, in preparation for a criminal case, I read a report which the investigating officer had composed for the Crown Attorney. "When I arrived at the building," this astute observer had recorded, "there were approximately two women in the hallway."

Another officer, reporting to his Crown Attorney, left this memorable passage for posterity:

"Constable Gamble, the breathalyzer technician, noted a very strong smell of liquor with a Ukrainian-type accent."

The folks at the Court House in Saint John, New Brunswick, are puzzled as to what to tell the man who recently sent this note: "I was married at your Court House 21st of December, 1978, and I was wondering if your office could send me a photocopy of my marriage consummation."

Why not tell him that the videotape hasn't come back yet from the last person to rent it?

Senior Judge Ed Kimelman, of the Manitoba Provincial Court (Family Division), received a letter from the principal of a Winnipeg high school, confirming that the judge would speak to the students about juvenile court. Judge Kimelman hadn't met the principal, but the last paragraph of the letter left him wondering just how much the fellow knew about him.

It read: "Our main purpose in our school credit course is to develop a healthy lifestyle. You will be able to show our students the results of an unhealthy lifestyle."

Bob Silk, of the Chartered Shorthand Reporters' Association of Ontario, reports that after unsuccessful efforts to settle a lawsuit, a lawyer received a letter from his opponent which read in part: "My client absolutely refuses to up his offer. Up yours."

And, speaking of letters, I reproduce below, in her own hand-writing, a letter scribbled by an elderly Canadian woman who wrote to thank a Mrs. Finch for sending her a radio. One day, when making her will, the woman had asked her lawyer if he could get her a radio to brighten her lonely days. The lawyer asked a friend, Mrs. Finch, if she would part with one of her radios, and she was pleased to oblige.

Here is the letter the donor received, exactly as written by the old woman, with only her signature and address deleted:

March 23, 1982

Dear Mrs Finch.

God bless you for giving your old radio to the Renee Lodge which in turn gave it to me. I have lived here in this nursing home since my dear husband passed on 12 years ago. I am 92 years old and never have any visitors anymore and I get so lonesome. Mrs Rogers who lives in the next room is 86 and she had a radio since she came here 5 year ago but would never let me listen to it. Yesterday her radio fell on the floor and broke so she asked if she could listen to mine and I said fuck you.

God bless you:

P.S.

Now wasn't that a lot of fun? We should do it again.

We *are* going to do it again, and this is your chance to deal yourself in on the hilarity.

If you have any true, humorous Canadian legal anecdotes you'd like to part with, send them along to me at the address shown below, immediately, if not sooner. Lawyers, judges, court reporters, newspaper reporters, policemen, legal secretaries – anyone with a yarn to spin is welcome.

Who knows? Your material might be "immortalized" in *More Court Jesters*.

PETER V. MacDONALD, Q.C.
302-10th Street
Hanover, Ontario
N4N 1P3

Contributors

Cyril J. Abbass — Toronto, Ont.

John Abbass — East Bay, N.S.

Judge Joseph L. Addison—Toronto, Ont.

Rosemary Aitken — Edmonton, Alta.

J. Trevor Alexander — Victoria, B.C.

Denis P. Archambault—Prince George, B.C.

B.K. Arlidge — Ottawa, Ont.

Mr. Justice John D. Arnup—Toronto, Ont.

Harry W. Arthurs — Toronto, Ont.

Douglas Baker — Burnaby, B.C.

George R. Baker — Ottawa, Ont.

John B. Ballem, Q.C. — Calgary, Alta.

Bill Barnett — Calgary, Alta.

R.A. Barr, Q.C. — Brockville, Ont.

John U. Bayly — Yellowknife, N.W.T.

Dorthea Beatie — Toronto, Ont.

Alan R. Bell — Winnipeg, Man.

Lewis A. Bell, Q.C. — Halifax, N.S.

Colin E. Bennett — Toronto, Ont.

Mr. Justice Anthime Bergeron— Montreal, Que.

S. Tupper Bigelow, Q.C.—Toronto, Ont.

Roger Bilodeau — Moncton, N.B.

Michael Blaxland — Vancouver, B.C.

Gordon J.Z. Bobesich — Sudbury, Ont.

Judge Michael G. Bolan—Brampton, Ont.

Barbara E. Bonham — Saint John, N.B.

Peter C. Bowal — Edmonton, Alta.

W.F. Bowker, Q.C. — Edmonton, Alta.

Mary E. Boyce — Toronto, Ont.

W.J. Lloyd Brennan, Q.C.—Ottawa, Ont.

Ronald H. Brooks—St. Catharines, Ont.

Thomas R. Brophey Jr.—Windsor, Ont.

Gerald C. Burke — Montreal, Que.

Martin H. Bushell, Q.C. — Halifax, N.S.

William E. Byers—Whitehorse, Yukon

Donald R. Cameron, Q.C.—Toronto, Ont.

A.G. Campbell, Q.C. — Toronto, Ont.

Ronald B. Cantlie, Q.C.—Winnipeg, Man.

John B. Carrel, Q.C.—Thunder Bay, Ont.

Kevin D. Carroll, Q.C. — Barrie, Ont.

Stephen C. Carter—Prince Albert, Sask.

Jane P. Cartwright — Kelowna, B.C.

W.G. Chappell — Richmond, B.C.

P.C. Chetty — Prince Albert, Sask.

David R. Chipman, Q.C.—Halifax, N.S.

Judge Gordon C. Chown—Hamilton, Ont.

Robert G. Church, Q.C.—Orangeville, Ont.

Steven R. Clark — Toronto, Ont.

R.A. Cluney, Q.C. — Halifax, N.S.

Hon. Thomas Coffin — Halifax, N.S.

David D. Conroy—North Battleford, Sask.

Hon. John S. Cormack—Edmonton, Alta.

Mona Cram — St. John's, Nfld.

Chief Justice Marcel Crête—Montreal, Que.

Ray Cuthbert — Toronto, Ont.

Maude Davis — Grand Prairie, Alta.

Roy W. Dawson — Dauphin, Man.

David C. Day, Q.C. — St. John's, Nfld.

Hilda Day — Sydney, N.S.

Robert G. De Bou — Vancouver, B.C.

Judge John A. Deacon—Brockville, Ont.

Mr. Justice Andre M. Dechene— Edmonton, Alta.

Betty Del Bianco — Kingston, Ont.

Robert M. Dick — Prince George, B.C.

Judge Eric C. Diehl — Melfort, Sask.

Gordon A. Douglas — Vancouver, B.C.

Judge M.L. Tyrwhitt-Drake—Victoria, B.C.

Judge Charles Drukarsh—Toronto, Ont.

Hon. J.L. Dubinsky — Halifax, N.S.

Mr. Justice Jacques Ducros — Montreal, Que.
Mike Duffy — Ottawa, Ont.
John G. Dunlop, Q.C. — New York, N.Y.
Mr. Justice W.R. DuPont — Toronto, Ont.
Robert E. Eades — Vancouver, B.C.
Keith E. Eaton, Q.C. — Chester Basin, N.S.
William M. Elliott, Q.C. — Regina, Sask.
Richard W. Elson — Saskatoon, Sask.
John A. Epp — Regina, Sask.
Mr. Justice Willard Z. Estey — Ottawa, Ont.
Chief Justice Gregory T. Evans — Toronto, Ont.
Lorna Farewell — St. John's, Nfld.
Brian R. Farmer — Walkerton, Ont.
Prof. Thomas G. Feeney, Q.C. — Ottawa, Ont.
Brian A. Felesky — Calgary, Alta.
Roderic G. Ferguson, Q.C. — Midland, Ont.
Maurice R. Fernandes — Toronto, Ont.
Judge Sam Filer — Brampton, Ont.
Judge F. Stewart Fisher — Islington, Ont.
S.G. Fisher, Q.C. — Toronto, Ont.
Rod J. Flaherty — Toronto, Ont.
Jim Flannery — Calgary, Alta.
Jennifer M. Foy — Calgary, Alta.
Arnold S. Fradkin — Ottawa, Ont.
Hon. Samuel Freedman, Q.C. — Winnipeg, Man.
Pierre Fournier — Montreal, Que.
David G. Friend, Q.C. — Toronto, Ont.
Patrick G. Furlong, Q.C. — Windsor, Ont.
Hon. George A. Gale — Toronto, Ont.
Robert W. Garcia — Hanover, Ont.
Adam W. Germain — Fort McMurray, Alta.
Prof. Dale Gibson — Winnipeg, Man.
T.J.K. Gillis, Q.C. — Sydney, N.S.
Mr. Justice Noel Goodridge — St. John's, Nfld.
Hon. Campbell Grant — Walkerton, Ont.

Lawrence Greenspon — Vanier, Ont.
Heather Griffiths — Orleans, Ont.
Robin Grigat — Edmonton, Alta.
G.T. Haig, Q.C. — Winnipeg, Man.
Hon. Emmett M. Hall, Q.C. — Saskatoon, Sask.
Robert R. Hall, Q.C. — Toronto, Ont.
Bruce J. Halliday — Calgary, Alta.
Don Hambling, Q.C. — Collingwood, Ont.
Patricia A. Hamilton — Weston, Ont.
J. Peter Hanes — London, Ont.
Mr. Justice John R. Hannan — Montreal, Que.
Mr. Justice A. Milton Harradence — Calgary, Alta.
Marg Harvey — Ottawa, Ont.
Rodney H. Hawkins — Williams Lake, B.C.
Strachan Heighington, Q.C. — Toronto, Ont.
Prof. R.G. Herbert, Q.C. — Vancouver, B.C.
Mr. Justice Robert J. Higgins — Saint John, N.B.
Tim J. Hilborn — Cambridge, Ont.
Philip Hiscock — St. John's, Nfld.
Robert L. Holden — Toronto, Ont.
John D. Honsberger, Q.C. — Toronto, Ont.
Judge Edward J. Houston — Ottawa, Ont.
Kenneth G. Houston, Q.C. — Winnipeg, Man.
Glen W. Howell — Toronto, Ont.
Tom Hubbard — Ottawa, Ont.
John L. Hughes — Toronto, Ont.
Kay Hughes — Winnipeg, Man.
Roydon A. Hughes, Q.C. — Ottawa, Ont.
Frederick R. Hume, Q.C. — Toronto, Ont.
J. Michael Hutchison — Victoria, B.C.
Constance D. Isherwood — Victoria, B.C.
Kenneth Jarvis, Q.C. — Toronto, Ont.
Doreen J. Johnson — Edmonton, Alberta

George A. Johnston, Q.C.—Toronto, Ont.

Louise M. Johnston—North Vancouver, B.C.

David I. Jones, Q.C.—Dartmouth, N.S.

William H. Jost, Q.C.—Annapolis Royal, N.S.

Mark Kawalsky — Midland, Ont.

Judge Harry J. Keenan—Brampton, Ont.

Terence V. Kelly, Q.C. — Oshawa, Ont.

Yvonne Kemp — Winnipeg, Man.

Judge James C. Kent—Brampton, Ont.

Donald A. Kerr, Q.C. — Halifax, N.S.

Vikas Khaladkar — Regina, Sask.

S.J. Khattar, Q.C. — Sydney, N.S.

Roman N. Komar — Toronto, Ont.

Rudy Kominek — Waterloo, Ont.

Mr. Justice Horace Krever—Toronto, Ont.

Boris Krivy, Q.C. — Toronto, Ont.

Serge Kujawa, Q.C. — Regina, Sask.

Joan Kurisko — Thunder Bay, Ont.

Gordon J. Kuski, Q.C.— Regina, Sask.

Alfred M. Kwinter — Toronto, Ont.

C. Ian Kyer — Toronto, Ont.

Marie E. Lalonde — Ottawa, Ont.

Hon. L.A. Landreville, Q.C.—Ottawa, Ont.

Judge Kenneth A. Langdon— Brampton, Ont.

C. Robert Langdon, Q.C.—Toronto, Ont.

J. Stuart Langford — Ottawa, Ont.

Norman Larsen — Winnipeg, Man.

D.G. Lawrence — Toronto, Ont.

Paul N. Leamen — Ottawa, Ont.

Lawrence Lebitka — Calgary, Alta.

Ronald J. LeBlanc — Moncton, N.B.

Kenneth P. Lefebvre, Q.C.—Brantford, Ont.

Judge Patrick LeSage — Toronto, Ont.

Ross B. Linton — Toronto, Ont.

J. Keith Lowes — Vancouver, B.C.

Judge Blake Lynch — Fredericton, N.B.

Chief Judge William D. Lyon— Toronto, Ont.

Alan H. MacDonald — Calgary, Alta.

Angus Norman MacDonald—Sydney, N.S.

Dan Alex MacDonald — Sydney, N.S.

Judge Ronald Angus MacDonald— Antigonish, N.S.

Mr. Justice Edward P. MacCallum— Edmonton, Alta.

Barbara MacGillivray—Edmonton, Alta.

Roderick G. MacGregor—Toronto, Ont.

Charles W. MacIntosh, Q.C.—Halifax, N.S.

Prof. Robert S. Mackay, Q.C.—London, Ont.

Judge Douglas MacKinnon— Vancouver, B.C.

Mr. Justice John H. Maher—Saskatoon, Sask.

Guy P. Major — Montreal, Que.

Arthur Maloney, Q.C. — Toronto, Ont.

Edward H. Masters — Ottawa, Ont.

J.A. Matheson — Edmonton, Alta.

David L. Mathieson, Q.C.—West Vancouver, B.C.

Kenneth M. Matthews, Q.C.—Truro, N.S.

Mr. Justice John W. McClung— Edmonton, Alta.

C.J. McCombe, Q.C. — Toronto, Ont.

Donald F. McCrimmon—Medicine Hat, Alta.

Judge Joseph McDonald—Kitchener, Ont.

John McDougall, Q.C.—Montreal, P.Q.

Chief Justice Allan McEachern— Vancouver, B.C.

Robert B. McGee, Q.C. — Toronto, Ont.

Gail McGilvray — Toronto, Ont.

E.J. McGrath — London, Ont.

Leo McIntyre — Glace Bay, N.S.

Robert D. McIntyre, Q.C.—Brampton, Ont.

Ed McKerroll — Toronto, Ont.

Colin D. McKinnon, Q.C.—Ottawa, Ont.

Richard D. McLean, Q.C.—Toronto, Ont.

Rod M. McLeod, Q.C. — Toronto, Ont.

Hon. Melvin J. McQuaid, Q.C. — Souris, P.E.I.

Ann McRae — Crystal City, Man.

Bob McVey — Toronto, Ont.

Murray G. Meldrum — Toronto, Ont.

Donald A. Mercer, Q.C. — St. John's, Nfld.

William R. Meredith, Q.C. — Ottawa, Ont.

Peter D. Messner — One Hundred Mile House, B.C.

Mr. Justice Pierre A. Michaud — Montreal, Que.

John H.E. Middlebro' — Owen Sound, Ont.

Maria Mihailovich — Hamilton, Ont.

Ralph S. Mills, Q.C. — Toronto, Ont.

Theresa C. Normandin-Mintzas — Montreal, Que.

John Palmer Moise, Q.C. — Toronto, Ont.

Mr. Justice R.A.F. Montgomery — Calgary, Alta.

Stephen Monty — Toronto, Ont.

Rene Monty — Key West, Fla.

Mr. Justice John W. Morden — Toronto, Ont.

Dr. Robert J. Morgan — Sydney, N.S.

Stuart Morrison — Toronto, Ont.

Judge Martin T. Morrissey — Brampton, Ont.

William G. Murphy — Toronto, Ont.

Mr. Justice George L. Murray — Vancouver, B.C.

Judge R.H. Mykle — Brandon, Man.

Chief Justice N.T. Nemetz — Vancouver, B.C.

Frank J. Newson — Edmonton, Alta.

Judge Peter Nicholson — Annapolis Royal, N.S.

Hon. Erik Nielsen, Q.C. — Ottawa, Ont.

Mr. Justice George E. Noble — Saskatoon, Sask.

Brendan O'Brien, Q.C. — Toronto, Ont.

Mr. Justice Michael O'Byrne — Edmonton, Alta.

Lester O'Donnell — Charlottetown, P.E.I.

Timothy J. O'Hara — Calgary, Alta.

C.E. Onley, Q.C. — North York, Ont.

Judge Seamus B. O'Regan — Goose Bay, Labrador, Nfld.

Mark M. Orkin, Q.C. — Toronto, Ont.

Judge P.B. Parker — Cobourg, Ont.

Eric J. Partridge — Victoria, B.C.

George Pate — Havelock, Ont.

Prof. Julien D. Payne, Q.C. — Ottawa, Ont.

J. Patrick Peacock, Q.C. — Calgary, Alta.

John J. Pepper, Q.C. — Montreal, Que.

Judge C. Emerson Perkins — Chatham, Ont.

Toomas Piliste — Delta, B.C.

Raymond L.D. du Plessis, Q.C. — Ottawa, Ont.

Howard Pontious — Kamloops, B.C.

Mr. Justice Joseph H. Potts — Toronto, Ont.

Denis J.R. Power, Q.C. — Ottawa, Ont.

Prof. Ronald R. Price, Q.C. — Kingston, Ont.

Ronald Price-Jones — Melfort, Sask.

Douglas H. Proudfoot, Q.C. — London, Ont.

Barbara Purvis — Vancouver, B.C.

Serge Radchuk, Q.C. — Winnipeg, Man.

Kenneth A. Rae, Q.C. — Owen Sound, Ont.

Bert Raphael, Q.C. — Toronto, Ont.

Moishe Reiter, Q.C. — Toronto, Ont.

Helen Rentis — Toronto, Ont.

David Roberts, Q.C. — Vancouver, B.C.

Peter A.B. Roberts — Vancouver, B.C.

John J. Robinette, Q.C. — Toronto, Ont.

Marthanne Robson — Toronto, Ont.

Arthur W. MacLeod Rogers, Q.C. — Victoria, B.C

Joseph Rosemin — Toronto, Ont.

C.M. Rosenblum, Q.C. — Sydney, N.S.

James D. Ross — Edmonton, Alta.

Patrick V. Rudden, Q.C. — Cornwall, Ont.

Manly S. Rusen — Winnipeg, Man.

A.B. Russ — Victoria, B.C.

Patrick A.A. Ryan, Q.C. — Fredericton, N.B.

Deedar Sagoo — Winnipeg, Man.

J.J. Saucier, Q.C. — Calgary, Alta.

Ronald J. Schmidt — West Vancouver, B.C.

Douglas S. Schofield — Kamloops, B.C.

Judge B. Barry Shapiro — Brampton, Ont.

Norman A. Shepherd, Q.C. — Kincardine, Ont.

Donna Sherbinin — Calgary, Alta.

Hal H. Sherwood — Cornwall, Ont.

Morris C. Shumiatcher, Q.C. — Regina, Sask.

Judge T.W. Shupe — Kamloops, B.C.

Bob Silk — Toronto, Ont.

Stan Smith — Scarborough, Ont.

Judge David Smout — London, England

J.L. Snith — Calgary, Alta.

Susie Sparks — Calgary, Alta.

Colin L. Spencer — Rosetown, Sask.

Sandra Spicer — Grande Prairie, Alta.

Christie Stone — Edmonton, Alta.

Marcel Strigberger — Toronto, Ont.

Roy St. George Stubbs — Winnipeg, Man.

Thomas R. Swabey — Cornwall, Ont.

Karen Swartzenberger — Edmonton, Alta.

Thomas Sylvester, Q.C. — Toronto, Ont.

Allan D. Thackray, Q.C. — Vancouver, B.C.

William L. Thatcher — Burlington, Ont.

Judge Donald G.E. Thompson — Barrie, Ont.

Claude R. Thomson — Toronto, Ont.

G. Ronald Toews — Smithers, B.C.

Orval J. Troy, Q.C. — Ottawa, Ont.

Hon. Walter A. Tucker, Q.C. — Saskatoon, Sask.

Mr. Justice William S. Tyndale — Montreal, Que.

J.L.K. Vamplew, Q.C. — Brockville, Ont.

Ellen J. Vezina — London, Ont.

Gunter Vordemberge — Toronto, Ont.

Mr. Justice Allan H. Wachowich — Edmonton, Alta.

Harvey G. Walker — North Battleford, Sask.

Mr. Justice George T. Walsh — Toronto, Ont.

Harry Walsh, Q.C. — Winnipeg, Man.

Donald J. Warner, Q.C. — Lindsay, Ont.

Mr. Justice M.M. de Weerdt — Whitehorse, Yukon

Judge Ernest F. West — Brampton, Ont.

Judge Walder G.W. White — Edmonton, Alta.

Edward C. Wildman — Barrie, Ont.

David R. Williams, Q.C. — Duncan, B.C.

Donald F. Woloshyn — North Battleford, Sask.

Sanford World, Q.C. — Toronto, Ont.